NORTH CAROLINA STATE PARKS & Historic Sites BUCKET JOURNAL

Explore the State Parks of North Carolina, USA

This book belongs to

_____

If found please call

_____

"**Of all the paths** you take in life, make sure a few of them are dirt" ~John Muir

"**We must remember** that North Carolina is more than a collection of regions and people. We are one state, one people, one family, bound by a common concern for each other. ~ Mike Easley

"**There in the highlands**, clear weather held for much of the time. The air lacked its usual haze, and the view stretched on and on across rows of blue mountains, each paler than the last until the final ranks were indistinguishable from the sky. It was as if all the world might be composed of nothing but valley and ridge."
~ Charles Frazier, Cold Mountain

NORTH CAROLINA STATE PARKS & Historic Sites BUCKET JOURNAL

©2020-2021 by My Bucket Journals LLC
Designed and printed in the USA. All rights reserved.

ISBN:
Published by My Bucket Journals, LLC
PO Box 310, Hutto, Texas 78634

This publication may not be reproduced stored or transmitted in whole or in part, in any form or by any means, electronic, mechanical or otherwise, without prior written consent from the publisher and author.

Brief quotations may be included in a review. If in PDF form, it may be stored on your computer and you may keep one online digital copy. This publication may be printed for personal use only.

Disclaimer
The information in this book is based on the author's opinion, knowledge and experience. The publisher and the author will not be held liable for the use or misuse of the information contained herein.

Disclosure
This book may contain affiliate links. If you click through an affiliate link to a third-party website and make a purchase, the author may receive a small commission.

Cover photo ©DepositPhotos

The State of North Carolina is a diverse state made up of mountains, foothills, and coastal seashores. With 322 miles of shoreline, 25 distinct beaches, and The Great Smoky Mountains, North Carolina has endless opportunities of fun for the whole family.

This breathtaking scenery encourages everyone who visits (or lives there) to get out and explore.

Some of the parks in the journal are well known and some are less traveled, all are waiting for you to discover their unique qualities.

In this North Carolina State Parks Bucket Journal, **you will find individual pages for 111 state parks, historic sites, beaches, and recreation areas** in the beautiful State of North Carolina. Many allow for overnight camping and all are great for day use trips.

This bucket journal is different. It gives you the ability to create your own unique exploration of whichever state park or historic site you choose.

How to Use Your North Carolina State Parks Bucket Journal

Parks that offer camping or other accommodations are on blue pages.
- Search out details about the state park or recreational site by using the website URL provided.
- Have fun planning the things you want to see on the left side of the 2-page spread.
- This is best done before you take your trip, but can be done while you are out exploring.
- On the right side, chronicle everything that you do and experience. Included is space for journaling and reflection about your stay in the park.

Parks that are Day Use Area Only are on purple pages.
- Day use parks are still fun to visit, even if you can't sleep there.
- Visit them when you are staying at other overnight parks or use them as day trip excursions to get out and explore.

The North Carolina State Parks Bucket Journal will become a living memory for your trips and adventures as you travel and discover the wonders of the state.

Enjoy exploring the beauty that is North Carolina!

TABLE OF CONTENTS

North Carolina Map 6
Coastal Region Parks...........7

Overnight Parks

- Goose Creek State Park........................ 8
- Bladen Lakes State Forest.................... 10
- Jones Lake State Park........................ 12
- Singletary Lake State Park.................. 14
- Lake Waccamaw State Park.................. 16
- Merchants Millpond State Park........... 18
- Carolina Beach State Park.................. 20
- Hammocks Beach State Park................ 22
- Pettigrew State Park......................... 24

Day Use Parks

- Historic Bath.................................. 26
- Brunswick Town / Fort Anderson Historic Site.................................. 27
- Dismal Swamp State Park................... 28
- Historic Edenton.............................. 29
- Tryon Palace Historic Site.................. 30
- Roanoke Island Festival Park HS.......... 31
- Jockeys Ridge State Park.................... 32
- CSS Neuse & Gov. Caswell Memorial Historic Site.................................. 33
- Fort Fisher State Rec. Area................. 34
- Fort Fisher State Historic Site.............. 35
- Battleship North Carolina HS.............. 36
- Somerset Place Historic Site.............. 37

Mountain Region Parks........39

Overnight Parks

- New River State Park......................... 40
- Stone Mountain State Park.................. 42
- Grandfather Mountain SP.................... 44
- Biltmore Estate.............................. 46
- South Mountains State Park................ 48
- Lake James State Park....................... 50
- Gorges State Park........................... 52
- Julian Price Memorial Park................. 54
- Mount Mitchell State Park.................. 56

Mountain Region Parks cont.

Day Use Parks

- Elk Knob State Park............................... 58
- Mount Jefferson State Park.................... 59
- Thomas Wolfe Memorial HS................... 60
- Zebulon B. Vance Birthplace HS.......... 61
- Chimney Rock State Park...................... 62
- Moses H Cone Memorial Park.............. 63
- Rendezvous Mountain Educational State Forest................................... 64

Piedmont Region Parks.........65

Overnight Parks

- Crowders Mountain State Park.............. 66
- Hanging Rock State Park....................... 68
- Boones Cave Park.............................. 70
- Eno River State Park.......................... 72
- Little River Regional Park & Natural Area................................... 74
- Haw River State Park.......................... 76
- Medoc Mountain State Park.................. 78
- Raven Rock State Park........................ 80
- Lake Norman State Park...................... 82
- Lumber River State Park...................... 84
- Mayo River State Park........................ 86
- Morrow Mountain State Park................ 88
- Pilot Mountain State Park.................... 90
- Kerr Lake State Recreation Area............ 92
- Jordan Lake State Rec. Area.................. 94
- William B Umstead State Park.............. 96
- Falls Lake State Rec. Area.................... 98
- Cliffs of the Neuse State Park.............. 100

Day Use Parks

- Reed Gold Mine Historic Site............... 102
- Carvers Creek State Park.................... 103
- Bennett Place Historic Site.................. 104

TABLE OF CONTENTS

Piedmont Region Parks cont.

- ❑ Duke Homestead Historic Site.............. 105
- ❑ Historic Stagville Historic Site.............. 106
- ❑ Alamance Battleground HS.................. 107
- ❑ Charlotte Hawkins Brown Museum Historic Site................................. 108
- ❑ Historic Halifax............................... 109
- ❑ Fort Dobbs Historic Site.................... 110
- ❑ Bentonville Battlefield HS..................111
- ❑ House in the Horseshoe HS................. 112
- ❑ President James K. Polk HS................. 113
- ❑ Town Creek Indian Mound HS................114
- ❑ Weymouth Woods Sandhills Nature Preserve...................................... 115
- ❑ Occoneechee Mountain State Natural Area.. 116
- ❑ North Carolina Transportation Museum....................................... 117
- ❑ Horne Creek Farm HS....................... 118
- ❑ N.C. State Capitol........................... 119
- ❑ Governor Charles B. Aycock Birthplace Historic Site................................. 120

Outer Banks Region.......121

Overnight Parks

- ❑ Rodanthe Beach............................. 122
- ❑ Waves Beach................................ 124
- ❑ Buxton Beach............................... 126
- ❑ Frisco Beach................................ 128
- ❑ Ocracoke Beach............................ 130

Day Use Parks

- ❑ Carova Beach............................... 132
- ❑ Currituck Nat. Wildlife Refuge............. 133
- ❑ Currituck Beach Lighthouse................. 134
- ❑ Corolla Beach............................... 135
- ❑ Duck Beach................................. 136
- ❑ Southern Shores Beach...................... 137
- ❑ Kitty Hawk Woods Coastal Reserve...................................... 138
- ❑ Kill Devil Hills.............................. 139
- ❑ Nags Head Beach........................... 140
- ❑ Manteo Island.............................. 141
- ❑ Wanchese Island............................ 142
- ❑ Cape Hatteras Nat. Seashore.............. 143

Outer Banks Region cont.

- ❑ Bodie Island Lighthouse..................... 144
- ❑ Pea Island Nat. Wildlife Refuge............ 145
- ❑ Salvo Day Use Area......................... 146
- ❑ Avon Beach................................. 147
- ❑ Cape Hatteras Lighthouse................... 148
- ❑ Hatteras Beach............................. 149
- ❑ Ocracoke Lighthouse........................ 150
- ❑ Portsmouth Island.......................... 151

Crystal Coast Region.......153

Overnight Parks

- ❑ Cedar Island............................... 154
- ❑ Harkers Island.............................. 156
- ❑ Beaufort.................................... 158
- ❑ Morehead City.............................. 160
- ❑ Emerald Isle................................ 162

Day Use Parks

- ❑ Cape Lookout Nat. Seashore............... 164
- ❑ Shackleford Banks.......................... 165
- ❑ Fort Macon State Park......................166
- ❑ Atlantic Beach.............................. 167
- ❑ Pine Knoll Shores........................... 168
- ❑ Theodore Roosevelt Nat. Area............169
- ❑ Indian Beach............................... 170

Add More Day Parks

- ❑ _____171
- ❑ _____172
- ❑ _____173
- ❑ _____174
- ❑ _____175
- ❑ _____176
- ❑ _____177

Add More Overnight Parks

- ❑ _____178
- ❑ _____180
- ❑ _____182

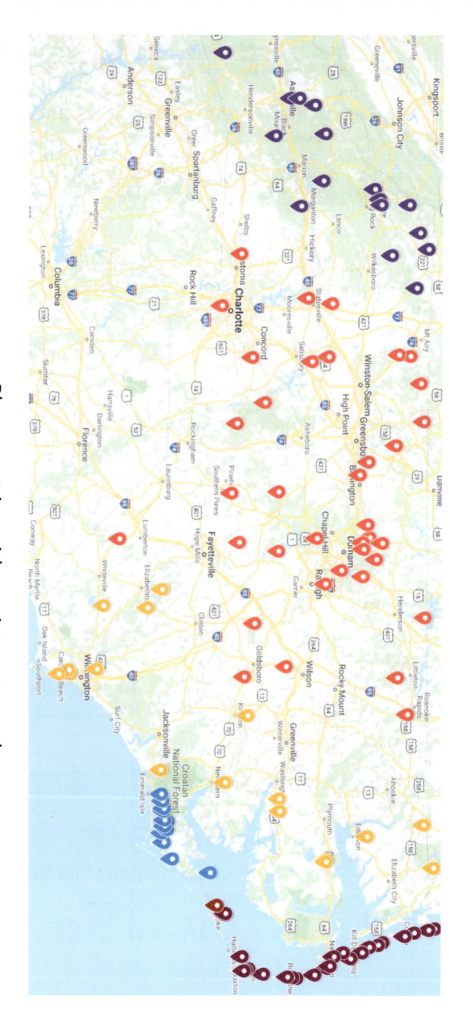

Plan your trips with our interact map!
Find it at https://cutt.ly/nc-state-parks

6

Goose Creek State Park
City: Camp Leach   County: Beaufort
Plan your trip: https://www.ncparks.gov/goose-creek-state-park/home

Activities:

- Biking
- Boating
- Disc Golf
- Fishing
- Gold Panning
- Hiking
- Historic Learning
- Horseback Riding
- Hunting
- Kite Boarding

- Metal Detecting
- OHV
- Paddling
- Rock Climbing
- Stargazing
- Swimming
- Wildlife Viewing
- Windsurfing

Facilities:

- ADA
- Picnic sites
- Restrooms
- Showers
- Trailer Access
- Visitor center
- Group Camping
- RV Camp
- Rustic Camping
- Cabins / Yurts
- Day Use Area

Notes:

Get the Facts

- Phone   252-923-2191
- Park Hours

  _____

- Reservations? ____Y ____N

  date made_____

- Open all year ____Y____N

  dates_____

- Check in time _____
- Check out time _____
- Pet friendly _____Y _____N
- Max RV length _____
- Distance from home

  miles: _____

  hours: _____

- Address_____

  _____

  _____

Fees:

- Day Use $ _____
- Camp Sites $ _____
- RV Sites $ _____
- Refund policy

  _____

  _____

  _____

Make It Personal

Trip dates:

The weather was: Sunny Cloudy Rainy Stormy Snowy Foggy Warm Cold

Why I went:

How I got there: (circle all that apply)   Plane   Train   Car   Bus   Bike   Hike   RV   MC

I went with:

We stayed in (space, cabin # etc):

Most relaxing day:

Something funny:

Someone we met:

Best story told:

The kids liked this:

The best food:

Games played:

Something disappointing:

Next time I'll do this differently:

Bladen Lakes State Forest
City: Elizabethtown   County: Bladen

Plan your trip: https://www.ncforestservice.gov/BladenLakes/index.htm

Activities:

- ☐ Biking
- ☐ Boating
- ☐ Disc Golf
- ☐ Fishing
- ☐ Gold Panning
- ☐ Hiking
- ☐ Historic Learning
- ☐ Horseback Riding
- ☐ Hunting
- ☐ Kite Boarding
- ☐ Metal Detecting
- ☐ OHV
- ☐ Paddling
- ☐ Rock Climbing
- ☐ Stargazing
- ☐ Swimming
- ☐ Wildlife Viewing
- ☐ Windsurfing
- ☐
- ☐
- ☐
- ☐
- ☐
- ☐
- ☐
- ☐
- ☐
- ☐
- ☐

Facilities:

- ☐ ADA
- ☐ Picnic sites
- ☐ Restrooms
- ☐ Showers
- ☐ Trailer Access
- ☐ Visitor center
- ☐ Group Camping
- ☐ RV Camp
- ☐ Rustic Camping
- ☐ Cabins / Yurts
- ☐ Day Use Area

Notes:

Get the Facts

- ☐ Phone   910-588-4964
- ☐ Park Hours

  _____

- ☐ Reservations? ____Y ____N

  date made_____
- ☐ Open all year ____Y_____N

  dates_____
- ☐ Check in time _____
- ☐ Check out time _____
- ☐ Pet friendly _____Y _____N
- ☐ Max RV length _____
- ☐ Distance from home

  miles: _____

  hours: _____
- ☐ Address_____

  _____

  _____

Fees:

- ☐ Day Use $ _____
- ☐ Camp Sites $ _____
- ☐ RV Sites $ _____
- ☐ Refund policy

  _____

  _____

  _____

Make It Personal

Trip dates: | The weather was: Sunny   Cloudy   Rainy   Stormy   Snowy   Foggy   Warm   Cold

Why I went:

How I got there: (circle all that apply)   Plane   Train   Car   Bus   Bike   Hike   RV   MC

I went with:

We stayed in (space, cabin # etc):

Most relaxing day:

Something funny:

Someone we met:

Best story told:

The kids liked this:

The best food:

Games played:

Something disappointing:

Next time I'll do this differently:

Jones Lake State Park
City: Elizabethtown   County: Bladen

Plan your trip: https://www.ncparks.gov/jones-lake-state-park/home

Activities:

- ❑ Biking
- ❑ Boating
- ❑ Disc Golf
- ❑ Fishing
- ❑ Gold Panning
- ❑ Hiking
- ❑ Historic Learning
- ❑ Horseback Riding
- ❑ Hunting
- ❑ Kite Boarding

- ❑ Metal Detecting
- ❑ OHV
- ❑ Paddling
- ❑ Rock Climbing
- ❑ Stargazing
- ❑ Swimming
- ❑ Wildlife Viewing
- ❑ Windsurfing
- ❑
- ❑

- ❑
- ❑
- ❑
- ❑
- ❑
- ❑
- ❑
- ❑
- ❑
- ❑

Facilities:

- ❑ ADA
- ❑ Picnic sites
- ❑ Restrooms
- ❑ Showers
- ❑ Trailer Access
- ❑ Visitor center
- ❑ Group Camping
- ❑ RV Camp
- ❑ Rustic Camping
- ❑ Cabins / Yurts
- ❑ Day Use Area

Notes:

Get the Facts

- ❑ Phone   910-588-4550
- ❑ Park Hours

  _____

- ❑ Reservations? ____Y ____N

  date made_____

- ❑ Open all year ____Y_____N

  dates_____

- ❑ Check in time _____
- ❑ Check out time _____
- ❑ Pet friendly _____Y _____N
- ❑ Max RV length _____
- ❑ Distance from home

  miles: _____

  hours: _____

- ❑ Address_____

  _____

  _____

Fees:

- ❑ Day Use $ _____
- ❑ Camp Sites $ _____
- ❑ RV Sites $ _____
- ❑ Refund policy

  _____

  _____

  _____

Make It Personal

Trip dates:

The weather was: Sunny Cloudy Rainy Stormy Snowy Foggy Warm Cold

Why I went:

How I got there: (circle all that apply) Plane Train Car Bus Bike Hike RV MC

I went with:

We stayed in (space, cabin # etc):

Most relaxing day:

Something funny:

Someone we met:

Best story told:

The kids liked this:

The best food:

Games played:

Something disappointing:

Next time I'll do this differently:

Singletary Lake State Park
City: Kelly   County: Bladen
Plan your trip: https://www.ncparks.gov/singletary-lake-state-park/home

Activities:

- ❑ Biking
- ❑ Boating
- ❑ Disc Golf
- ❑ Fishing
- ❑ Gold Panning
- ❑ Hiking
- ❑ Historic Learning
- ❑ Horseback Riding
- ❑ Hunting
- ❑ Kite Boarding
- ❑ Metal Detecting
- ❑ OHV
- ❑ Paddling
- ❑ Rock Climbing
- ❑ Stargazing
- ❑ Swimming
- ❑ Wildlife Viewing
- ❑ Windsurfing
- ❑
- ❑

Facilities:

- ❑ ADA
- ❑ Picnic sites
- ❑ Restrooms
- ❑ Showers
- ❑ Trailer Access
- ❑ Visitor center
- ❑ Group Camping
- ❑ RV Camp
- ❑ Rustic Camping
- ❑ Cabins / Yurts
- ❑ Day Use Area

Notes:

Get the Facts

- ❑ Phone   910-669-2928
- ❑ Park Hours

  _____

- ❑ Reservations? ____Y ____N

  date made_____

- ❑ Open all year ____Y____N

  dates_____

- ❑ Check in time _____

- ❑ Check out time _____

- ❑ Pet friendly _____Y _____N

- ❑ Max RV length _____

- ❑ Distance from home

  miles: _____

  hours: _____

- ❑ Address_____

  _____

  _____

Fees:

- ❑ Day Use $ _____
- ❑ Camp Sites $ _____
- ❑ RV Sites $ _____
- ❑ Refund policy

  _____

  _____

  _____

Make It Personal

Trip dates:

The weather was: Sunny Cloudy Rainy Stormy Snowy Foggy Warm Cold

Why I went:

How I got there: (circle all that apply) Plane Train Car Bus Bike Hike RV MC

I went with:

We stayed in (space, cabin # etc):

Most relaxing day:

Something funny:

Someone we met:

Best story told:

The kids liked this:

The best food:

Games played:

Something disappointing:

Next time I'll do this differently:

Lake Waccamaw State Park
City: State Park   County: Carteret
Plan your trip: https://www.ncparks.gov/lake-waccamaw-state-park/home

Activities:

- ❑ Biking
- ❑ Boating
- ❑ Disc Golf
- ❑ Fishing
- ❑ Gold Panning
- ❑ Hiking
- ❑ Historic Learning
- ❑ Horseback Riding
- ❑ Hunting
- ❑ Kite Boarding

- ❑ Metal Detecting
- ❑ OHV
- ❑ Paddling
- ❑ Rock Climbing
- ❑ Stargazing
- ❑ Swimming
- ❑ Wildlife Viewing
- ❑ Windsurfing
- ❑
- ❑

- ❑
- ❑
- ❑
- ❑
- ❑
- ❑
- ❑
- ❑
- ❑
- ❑

Facilities:

- ❑ ADA
- ❑ Picnic sites
- ❑ Restrooms
- ❑ Showers
- ❑ Trailer Access
- ❑ Visitor center
- ❑ Group Camping
- ❑ RV Camp
- ❑ Rustic Camping
- ❑ Cabins / Yurts
- ❑ Day Use Area

Notes:

Get the Facts

- ❑ Phone   910-646-4748
- ❑ Park Hours

  _____

- ❑ Reservations? _____Y _____N

  date made_____

- ❑ Open all year _____Y_____N

  dates_____

- ❑ Check in time _____
- ❑ Check out time _____
- ❑ Pet friendly _____Y _____N
- ❑ Max RV length _____
- ❑ Distance from home

  miles: _____

  hours: _____

- ❑ Address_____

  _____

  _____

Fees:

- ❑ Day Use $ _____
- ❑ Camp Sites $ _____
- ❑ RV Sites $ _____
- ❑ Refund policy

  _____

  _____

  _____

Make It Personal

Trip dates:

The weather was: Sunny Cloudy Rainy Stormy Snowy Foggy Warm Cold

Why I went:

How I got there: (circle all that apply) Plane Train Car Bus Bike Hike RV MC

I went with:

We stayed in (space, cabin # etc):

Most relaxing day:

Something funny:

Someone we met:

Best story told:

The kids liked this:

The best food:

Games played:

Something disappointing:

Next time I'll do this differently:

Merchants Millpond State Park
City: Millpond Road   County: Gates

Plan your trip: https://www.ncparks.gov/merchants-millpond-state-park/home

Activities:

- ❏ Biking
- ❏ Boating
- ❏ Disc Golf
- ❏ Fishing
- ❏ Gold Panning
- ❏ Hiking
- ❏ Historic Learning
- ❏ Horseback Riding
- ❏ Hunting
- ❏ Kite Boarding

- ❏ Metal Detecting
- ❏ OHV
- ❏ Paddling
- ❏ Rock Climbing
- ❏ Stargazing
- ❏ Swimming
- ❏ Wildlife Viewing
- ❏ Windsurfing
- ❏
- ❏

- ❏
- ❏
- ❏
- ❏
- ❏
- ❏
- ❏
- ❏
- ❏
- ❏

Facilities:

- ❏ ADA
- ❏ Picnic sites
- ❏ Restrooms
- ❏ Showers
- ❏ Trailer Access
- ❏ Visitor center
- ❏ Group Camping
- ❏ RV Camp
- ❏ Rustic Camping
- ❏ Cabins / Yurts
- ❏ Day Use Area

Notes:

Get the Facts

- ❏ Phone   252-357-1191
- ❏ Park Hours

  _____

- ❏ Reservations? ____Y ____N

  date made_____

- ❏ Open all year ____Y____N

  dates_____

- ❏ Check in time _____

- ❏ Check out time _____

- ❏ Pet friendly _____Y _____N

- ❏ Max RV length _____

- ❏ Distance from home

  miles: _____

  hours: _____

- ❏ Address_____

  _____

  _____

Fees:

- ❏ Day Use $ _____
- ❏ Camp Sites $ _____
- ❏ RV Sites $ _____
- ❏ Refund policy

  _____

  _____

  _____

Make It Personal

Trip dates:

The weather was: Sunny Cloudy Rainy Stormy Snowy Foggy Warm Cold

Why I went:

How I got there: (circle all that apply) Plane Train Car Bus Bike Hike RV MC

I went with:

We stayed in (space, cabin # etc):

Most relaxing day:

Something funny:

Someone we met:

Best story told:

The kids liked this:

The best food:

Games played:

Something disappointing:

Next time I'll do this differently:

Carolina Beach State Park
City: Carolina Beach   County: New Hanover

Plan your trip: https://www.ncparks.gov/carolina-beach-state-park/home

Activities:

- ❑ Biking
- ❑ Boating
- ❑ Disc Golf
- ❑ Fishing
- ❑ Gold Panning
- ❑ Hiking
- ❑ Historic Learning
- ❑ Horseback Riding
- ❑ Hunting
- ❑ Kite Boarding
- ❑ Metal Detecting
- ❑ OHV
- ❑ Paddling
- ❑ Rock Climbing
- ❑ Stargazing
- ❑ Swimming
- ❑ Wildlife Viewing
- ❑ Windsurfing
- ❑
- ❑
- ❑
- ❑
- ❑
- ❑
- ❑
- ❑
- ❑
- ❑
- ❑

Facilities:

- ❑ ADA
- ❑ Picnic sites
- ❑ Restrooms
- ❑ Showers
- ❑ Trailer Access
- ❑ Visitor center
- ❑ Group Camping
- ❑ RV Camp
- ❑ Rustic Camping
- ❑ Cabins / Yurts
- ❑ Day Use Area

Notes:

Get the Facts

- ❑ Phone   910-458-8206
- ❑ Park Hours

  _____

- ❑ Reservations? _____Y _____N

  date made_____

- ❑ Open all year _____Y_____N

  dates_____

- ❑ Check in time _____
- ❑ Check out time _____
- ❑ Pet friendly _____Y _____N
- ❑ Max RV length _____
- ❑ Distance from home

  miles: _____

  hours: _____

- ❑ Address_____

  _____

  _____

Fees:

- ❑ Day Use $ _____
- ❑ Camp Sites $ _____
- ❑ RV Sites $ _____
- ❑ Refund policy

  _____

  _____

  _____

Make It Personal

Trip dates:

The weather was: Sunny Cloudy Rainy Stormy Snowy Foggy Warm Cold

Why I went:

How I got there: (circle all that apply) Plane Train Car Bus Bike Hike RV MC

I went with:

We stayed in (space, cabin # etc):

Most relaxing day:

Something funny:

Someone we met:

Best story told:

The kids liked this:

The best food:

Games played:

Something disappointing:

Next time I'll do this differently:

Hammocks Beach State Park
City: Swansboro   County: Onslow

Plan your trip: https://www.ncparks.gov/hammocks-beach-state-park/home

Activities:

- ❑ Biking
- ❑ Boating
- ❑ Disc Golf
- ❑ Fishing
- ❑ Gold Panning
- ❑ Hiking
- ❑ Historic Learning
- ❑ Horseback Riding
- ❑ Hunting
- ❑ Kite Boarding

- ❑ Metal Detecting
- ❑ OHV
- ❑ Paddling
- ❑ Rock Climbing
- ❑ Stargazing
- ❑ Swimming
- ❑ Wildlife Viewing
- ❑ Windsurfing

- ❑
- ❑
- ❑
- ❑
- ❑
- ❑
- ❑
- ❑
- ❑
- ❑

Facilities:

- ❑ ADA
- ❑ Picnic sites
- ❑ Restrooms
- ❑ Showers
- ❑ Trailer Access
- ❑ Visitor center
- ❑ Group Camping
- ❑ RV Camp
- ❑ Rustic Camping
- ❑ Cabins / Yurts
- ❑ Day Use Area

Notes:

Get the Facts

- ❑ Phone   910-326-4881
- ❑ Park Hours

  _____

- ❑ Reservations? _____ Y _____ N

  date made_____

- ❑ Open all year _____ Y _____ N

  dates_____

- ❑ Check in time _____
- ❑ Check out time _____
- ❑ Pet friendly _____ Y _____ N
- ❑ Max RV length _____
- ❑ Distance from home

  miles: _____

  hours: _____

- ❑ Address_____

  _____

  _____

Fees:

- ❑ Day Use $ _____
- ❑ Camp Sites $ _____
- ❑ RV Sites $ _____
- ❑ Refund policy

  _____

  _____

  _____

Make It Personal

Trip dates:

The weather was: Sunny Cloudy Rainy Stormy Snowy Foggy Warm Cold

Why I went:

How I got there: (circle all that apply) Plane Train Car Bus Bike Hike RV MC

I went with:

We stayed in (space, cabin # etc):

Most relaxing day:

Something funny:

Someone we met:

Best story told:

The kids liked this:

The best food:

Games played:

Something disappointing:

Next time I'll do this differently:

23

Pettigrew State Park
City: Creswell   County: Washington

Plan your trip: https://www.ncparks.gov/pettigrew-state-park/home

Activities:

- ❑ Biking
- ❑ Boating
- ❑ Disc Golf
- ❑ Fishing
- ❑ Gold Panning
- ❑ Hiking
- ❑ Historic Learning
- ❑ Horseback Riding
- ❑ Hunting
- ❑ Kite Boarding

- ❑ Metal Detecting
- ❑ OHV
- ❑ Paddling
- ❑ Rock Climbing
- ❑ Stargazing
- ❑ Swimming
- ❑ Wildlife Viewing
- ❑ Windsurfing
- ❑
- ❑

- ❑
- ❑
- ❑
- ❑
- ❑
- ❑
- ❑
- ❑
- ❑
- ❑

Facilities:

- ❑ ADA
- ❑ Picnic sites
- ❑ Restrooms
- ❑ Showers
- ❑ Trailer Access
- ❑ Visitor center
- ❑ Group Camping
- ❑ RV Camp
- ❑ Rustic Camping
- ❑ Cabins / Yurts
- ❑ Day Use Area

Notes:

Get the Facts

- ❑ Phone   252-797-4475
- ❑ Park Hours

_____

- ❑ Reservations? ____Y ____N

date made_____

- ❑ Open all year ____Y ____N

dates_____

- ❑ Check in time _____
- ❑ Check out time _____
- ❑ Pet friendly _____Y _____N
- ❑ Max RV length _____
- ❑ Distance from home

miles: _____

hours: _____

- ❑ Address_____

_____

_____

Fees:

- ❑ Day Use $ _____
- ❑ Camp Sites $ _____
- ❑ RV Sites $ _____
- ❑ Refund policy

_____

_____

_____

Make It Personal

Trip dates:

The weather was: Sunny Cloudy Rainy Stormy Snowy Foggy Warm Cold

Why I went:

How I got there: (circle all that apply)   Plane   Train   Car   Bus   Bike   Hike   RV   MC

I went with:

We stayed in (space, cabin # etc):

Most relaxing day:

Something funny:

Someone we met:

Best story told:

The kids liked this:

The best food:

Games played:

Something disappointing:

Next time I'll do this differently:

Historic Bath
City: Bath   County: Beaufort

Plan your trip: https://historicsites.nc.gov/node/56

Activities:

- ❑ ATV / OHV   ❑
- ❑ Bike Trails   ❑
- ❑ Birding   ❑
- ❑ Boating   ❑
- ❑ Fishing   ❑
- ❑ Hiking   ❑
- ❑ Horseback   ❑
- ❑ Mountain Biking   ❑
- ❑ Watersports   ❑
- ❑ Wildlife   ❑
- ❑ Winter Sports

Facilities:

- ❑ ADA   ❑
- ❑ Gift Shop   ❑
- ❑ Museum   ❑
- ❑ Visitor Center   ❑
- ❑ Picnic sites   ❑
- ❑ Restrooms   ❑

Things to do in the area:

Get the Facts

- ❑ Phone 252-923-3971
- ❑ Park Hours

  _____

- ❑ Reservations? ____Y ____N

  date made_____

- ❑ Open all year? ____Y____N

  dates_____

- ❑ Dog friendly _____Y _____N

- ❑ Distance from home

  miles: _____

  hours: _____

- ❑ Address_____

  _____

  _____

Fees:

- ❑ Day Use $ _____
- ❑ Refund policy

  _____

  _____

  _____

Notes:

Brunswick Town / Fort Anderson Historic Site

City: Winnabow   County: Brunswick

Plan your trip: https://historicsites.nc.gov/node/50

Activities:

- ☐ ATV / OHV   ☐
- ☐ Bike Trails   ☐
- ☐ Birding   ☐
- ☐ Boating   ☐
- ☐ Fishing   ☐
- ☐ Hiking   ☐
- ☐ Horseback   ☐
- ☐ Mountain Biking   ☐
- ☐ Watersports   ☐
- ☐ Wildlife   ☐
- ☐ Winter Sports

Facilities:

- ☐ ADA   ☐
- ☐ Gift Shop   ☐
- ☐ Museum   ☐
- ☐ Visitor Center   ☐
- ☐ Picnic sites   ☐
- ☐ Restrooms   ☐

Things to do in the area:

Get the Facts

- ☐ Phone 910-371-6613
- ☐ Park Hours

  _____

- ☐ Reservations? ____Y ____N

  date made_____

- ☐ Open all year? ____Y____N

  dates_____

- ☐ Dog friendly _____Y _____N

- ☐ Distance from home

  miles: _____

  hours: _____

- ☐ Address_____

  _____

  _____

Fees:

- ☐ Day Use $ _____
- ☐ Refund policy

  _____

  _____

  _____

Notes:

Dismal Swamp State Park
City: South Mills   County: Camden

Plan your trip: https://www.ncparks.gov/dismal-swamp-state-park/home

Activities:

- [ ] ATV / OHV
- [ ] Bike Trails
- [ ] Birding
- [ ] Boating
- [ ] Fishing
- [ ] Hiking
- [ ] Horseback
- [ ] Mountain Biking
- [ ] Watersports
- [ ] Wildlife
- [ ] Winter Sports

- [ ]
- [ ]
- [ ]
- [ ]
- [ ]
- [ ]
- [ ]
- [ ]
- [ ]
- [ ]

Facilities:

- [ ] ADA
- [ ] Gift Shop
- [ ] Museum
- [ ] Visitor Center
- [ ] Picnic sites
- [ ] Restrooms

- [ ]
- [ ]
- [ ]
- [ ]
- [ ]
- [ ]

Things to do in the area:

Get the Facts

- [ ] Phone 252-771-6593
- [ ] Park Hours

  _____

- [ ] Reservations? ____Y ____N

  date made_____

- [ ] Open all year? ____Y____N

  dates_____

- [ ] Dog friendly _____Y _____N

- [ ] Distance from home

  miles: _____

  hours: _____

- [ ] Address_____

  _____

  _____

Fees:

- [ ] Day Use $ _____
- [ ] Refund policy

  _____

  _____

  _____

Notes:

Historic Edenton

City: Edenton   County: Chowan

Plan your trip: https://historicsites.nc.gov/node/57

Activities:

- ❑ ATV / OHV   ❑
- ❑ Bike Trails   ❑
- ❑ Birding   ❑
- ❑ Boating   ❑
- ❑ Fishing   ❑
- ❑ Hiking   ❑
- ❑ Horseback   ❑
- ❑ Mountain Biking   ❑
- ❑ Watersports   ❑
- ❑ Wildlife   ❑
- ❑ Winter Sports

Facilities:

- ❑ ADA   ❑
- ❑ Gift Shop   ❑
- ❑ Museum   ❑
- ❑ Visitor Center   ❑
- ❑ Picnic sites   ❑
- ❑ Restrooms   ❑

Things to do in the area:

Get the Facts

- ❑ Phone 252-482-2637
- ❑ Park Hours

  _____

- ❑ Reservations? _____Y _____N

  date made_____

- ❑ Open all year? _____Y_____N

  dates_____

- ❑ Dog friendly _____Y _____N

- ❑ Distance from home

  miles: _____

  hours: _____

- ❑ Address_____

  _____

  _____

Fees:

- ❑ Day Use $ _____
- ❑ Refund policy

  _____

  _____

  _____

Notes:

Tryon Palace Historic Site
City: New Bern   County: Craven

Plan your trip: https://www.tryonpalace.org/

Activities:

- ❑ ATV / OHV   ❑
- ❑ Bike Trails   ❑
- ❑ Birding   ❑
- ❑ Boating   ❑
- ❑ Fishing   ❑
- ❑ Hiking   ❑
- ❑ Horseback   ❑
- ❑ Mountain Biking   ❑
- ❑ Watersports   ❑
- ❑ Wildlife   ❑
- ❑ Winter Sports

Facilities:

- ❑ ADA   ❑
- ❑ Gift Shop   ❑
- ❑ Museum   ❑
- ❑ Visitor Center   ❑
- ❑ Picnic sites   ❑
- ❑ Restrooms   ❑

Things to do in the area:

Get the Facts

- ❑ Phone 800-767-1560
- ❑ Park Hours

  _____

- ❑ Reservations? ____Y ____N

  date made_____

- ❑ Open all year? ____Y____N

  dates_____

- ❑ Dog friendly _____Y _____N

- ❑ Distance from home

  miles: _____

  hours: _____

- ❑ Address_____

  _____

  _____

Fees:

- ❑ Day Use $ _____
- ❑ Refund policy

  _____

  _____

  _____

Notes:

Roanoke Island Festival Park Historic Site

City: Manteo   County: Dare

Plan your trip: https://www.roanokeisland.com/

Activities:

- ☐ ATV / OHV   ☐
- ☐ Bike Trails   ☐
- ☐ Birding   ☐
- ☐ Boating   ☐
- ☐ Fishing   ☐
- ☐ Hiking   ☐
- ☐ Horseback   ☐
- ☐ Mountain Biking   ☐
- ☐ Watersports   ☐
- ☐ Wildlife   ☐
- ☐ Winter Sports

Facilities:

- ☐ ADA   ☐
- ☐ Gift Shop   ☐
- ☐ Museum   ☐
- ☐ Visitor Center   ☐
- ☐ Picnic sites   ☐
- ☐ Restrooms   ☐

Things to do in the area:

Get the Facts

- ☐ Phone 252-475-1500
- ☐ Park Hours

  _____

- ☐ Reservations? ____Y ____N

  date made_____

- ☐ Open all year? ____Y____N

  dates_____

- ☐ Dog friendly _____Y _____N

- ☐ Distance from home

  miles: _____

  hours: _____

- ☐ Address_____

  _____

  _____

Fees:

- ☐ Day Use $ _____
- ☐ Refund policy

  _____

  _____

  _____

Notes:

Jockeys Ridge State Park
City: Nags Head   County: Dare

Plan your trip: https://www.ncparks.gov/jockeys-ridge-state-park/home

Activities:

- ❑ ATV / OHV   ❑
- ❑ Bike Trails   ❑
- ❑ Birding   ❑
- ❑ Boating   ❑
- ❑ Fishing   ❑
- ❑ Hiking   ❑
- ❑ Horseback   ❑
- ❑ Mountain Biking   ❑
- ❑ Watersports   ❑
- ❑ Wildlife   ❑
- ❑ Winter Sports

Facilities:

- ❑ ADA   ❑
- ❑ Gift Shop   ❑
- ❑ Museum   ❑
- ❑ Visitor Center   ❑
- ❑ Picnic sites   ❑
- ❑ Restrooms   ❑

Things to do in the area:

Get the Facts

- ❑ Phone 252-441-7132
- ❑ Park Hours

_____

- ❑ Reservations? _____Y _____N

date made_____

- ❑ Open all year? _____Y_____N

dates_____

- ❑ Dog friendly _____Y _____N
- ❑ Distance from home

miles: _____

hours: _____

- ❑ Address_____

_____

_____

Fees:

- ❑ Day Use $ _____
- ❑ Refund policy

_____

_____

_____

Notes:

CSS Neuse & Gov. Caswell Memorial Historic Site

City: Kinston   County: Lenoir

Plan your trip: https://historicsites.nc.gov/all-sites/css-neuse-and-governor-caswell-memorial

Activities:

- ❑ ATV / OHV   ❑
- ❑ Bike Trails   ❑
- ❑ Birding   ❑
- ❑ Boating   ❑
- ❑ Fishing   ❑
- ❑ Hiking   ❑
- ❑ Horseback   ❑
- ❑ Mountain Biking   ❑
- ❑ Watersports   ❑
- ❑ Wildlife   ❑
- ❑ Winter Sports

Facilities:

- ❑ ADA   ❑
- ❑ Gift Shop   ❑
- ❑ Museum   ❑
- ❑ Visitor Center   ❑
- ❑ Picnic sites   ❑
- ❑ Restrooms   ❑

Things to do in the area:

Get the Facts

- ❑ Phone 252-522-2107
- ❑ Park Hours

    _____

- ❑ Reservations? _____Y _____N

    date made_____

- ❑ Open all year? _____Y_____N

    dates_____

- ❑ Dog friendly _____Y _____N

- ❑ Distance from home

    miles: _____

    hours: _____

- ❑ Address_____

    _____

    _____

Fees:

- ❑ Day Use $ _____
- ❑ Refund policy

    _____

    _____

    _____

Notes:

Fort Fisher State Recreation Area
City: Kure Beach   County: New Hanover

Plan your trip: https://www.ncparks.gov/fort-fisher-state-recreation-area/home

Activities:

- ❑ ATV / OHV   ❑
- ❑ Bike Trails   ❑
- ❑ Birding   ❑
- ❑ Boating   ❑
- ❑ Fishing   ❑
- ❑ Hiking   ❑
- ❑ Horseback   ❑
- ❑ Mountain Biking   ❑
- ❑ Watersports   ❑
- ❑ Wildlife   ❑
- ❑ Winter Sports

Facilities:

- ❑ ADA   ❑
- ❑ Gift Shop   ❑
- ❑ Museum   ❑
- ❑ Visitor Center   ❑
- ❑ Picnic sites   ❑
- ❑ Restrooms   ❑

Things to do in the area:

Get the Facts

- ❑ Phone 910-458-5798
- ❑ Park Hours

  _____

- ❑ Reservations? _____Y _____N

  date made_____

- ❑ Open all year? _____Y_____N

  dates_____

- ❑ Dog friendly _____Y _____N

- ❑ Distance from home

  miles: _____

  hours: _____

- ❑ Address_____

  _____

  _____

Fees:

- ❑ Day Use $ _____
- ❑ Refund policy

  _____

  _____

  _____

Notes:

Fort Fisher State Historic Site
City: Kure Beach   County: New Hanover
Plan your trip: https://www.ncparks.gov/fort-fisher-state-recreation-area/home

Activities:

- ❑ ATV / OHV   ❑
- ❑ Bike Trails   ❑
- ❑ Birding   ❑
- ❑ Boating   ❑
- ❑ Fishing   ❑
- ❑ Hiking   ❑
- ❑ Horseback   ❑
- ❑ Mountain Biking   ❑
- ❑ Watersports   ❑
- ❑ Wildlife   ❑
- ❑ Winter Sports

Facilities:

- ❑ ADA   ❑
- ❑ Gift Shop   ❑
- ❑ Museum   ❑
- ❑ Visitor Center   ❑
- ❑ Picnic sites   ❑
- ❑ Restrooms   ❑

Things to do in the area:

Get the Facts

- ❑ Phone 910-458-5798
- ❑ Park Hours

  _____

- ❑ Reservations? ____Y ____N

  date made_____

- ❑ Open all year? ____Y____N

  dates_____

- ❑ Dog friendly _____Y _____N

- ❑ Distance from home

  miles: _____

  hours: _____

- ❑ Address_____

  _____

  _____

Fees:

- ❑ Day Use $ _____
- ❑ Refund policy

  _____
  _____
  _____

Notes:

Battleship North Carolina Historic Site
City: Wilmington   County: New Hanover
Plan your trip: http://www.battleshipnc.com/

Activities:

- ❏ ATV / OHV   ❏
- ❏ Bike Trails   ❏
- ❏ Birding   ❏
- ❏ Boating   ❏
- ❏ Fishing   ❏
- ❏ Hiking   ❏
- ❏ Horseback   ❏
- ❏ Mountain Biking   ❏
- ❏ Watersports   ❏
- ❏ Wildlife   ❏
- ❏ Winter Sports

Facilities:

- ❏ ADA   ❏
- ❏ Gift Shop   ❏
- ❏ Museum   ❏
- ❏ Visitor Center   ❏
- ❏ Picnic sites   ❏
- ❏ Restrooms   ❏

Things to do in the area:

Get the Facts

- ❏ Phone 910-399-9100
- ❏ Park Hours

  _____

- ❏ Reservations? _____Y _____N

  date made_____

- ❏ Open all year? _____Y_____N

  dates_____

- ❏ Dog friendly _____Y _____N

- ❏ Distance from home

  miles: _____

  hours: _____

- ❏ Address_____

  _____

  _____

Fees:

- ❏ Day Use $ _____
- ❏ Refund policy

  _____

  _____

  _____

Notes:

Somerset Place Historic Site
City: Creswell   County: Washington
Plan your trip: https://historicsites.nc.gov/node/66

Activities:

- ❏ ATV / OHV   ❏
- ❏ Bike Trails   ❏
- ❏ Birding   ❏
- ❏ Boating   ❏
- ❏ Fishing   ❏
- ❏ Hiking   ❏
- ❏ Horseback   ❏
- ❏ Mountain Biking   ❏
- ❏ Watersports   ❏
- ❏ Wildlife   ❏
- ❏ Winter Sports

Facilities:

- ❏ ADA   ❏
- ❏ Gift Shop   ❏
- ❏ Museum   ❏
- ❏ Visitor Center   ❏
- ❏ Picnic sites   ❏
- ❏ Restrooms   ❏

Things to do in the area:

Get the Facts

- ❏ Phone 252-797-4560
- ❏ Park Hours

  _____

- ❏ Reservations? _____Y _____N

  date made_____

- ❏ Open all year? _____Y_____N

  dates_____

- ❏ Dog friendly _____Y _____N

- ❏ Distance from home

  miles: _____

  hours: _____

- ❏ Address_____

  _____

  _____

Fees:

- ❏ Day Use $ _____
- ❏ Refund policy

  _____

  _____

  _____

Notes:

Notes:

New River State Park
City: Laurel Springs   County: Alleghany

Plan your trip: https://www.ncparks.gov/new-river-state-park/home

Activities:

- ❑ Biking
- ❑ Boating
- ❑ Disc Golf
- ❑ Fishing
- ❑ Gold Panning
- ❑ Hiking
- ❑ Historic Learning
- ❑ Horseback Riding
- ❑ Hunting
- ❑ Kite Boarding

- ❑ Metal Detecting
- ❑ OHV
- ❑ Paddling
- ❑ Rock Climbing
- ❑ Stargazing
- ❑ Swimming
- ❑ Wildlife Viewing
- ❑ Windsurfing
- ❑
- ❑

- ❑
- ❑
- ❑
- ❑
- ❑
- ❑
- ❑
- ❑
- ❑
- ❑

Facilities:

- ❑ ADA
- ❑ Picnic sites
- ❑ Restrooms
- ❑ Showers
- ❑ Trailer Access
- ❑ Visitor center
- ❑ Group Camping
- ❑ RV Camp
- ❑ Rustic Camping
- ❑ Cabins / Yurts
- ❑ Day Use Area

Notes:

Get the Facts

- ❑ Phone   336-982-2587
- ❑ Park Hours

  _____

- ❑ Reservations? ____Y ____N

  date made_____
- ❑ Open all year ____Y____N

  dates_____
- ❑ Check in time _____
- ❑ Check out time _____
- ❑ Pet friendly _____Y _____N
- ❑ Max RV length _____
- ❑ Distance from home

  miles: _____

  hours: _____
- ❑ Address_____

  _____

  _____

Fees:

- ❑ Day Use $ _____
- ❑ Camp Sites $ _____
- ❑ RV Sites $ _____
- ❑ Refund policy

  _____

  _____

  _____

Make It Personal

Trip dates:

The weather was: Sunny Cloudy Rainy Stormy Snowy Foggy Warm Cold

Why I went:

How I got there: (circle all that apply) Plane Train Car Bus Bike Hike RV MC

I went with:

We stayed in (space, cabin # etc):

Most relaxing day:

Something funny:

Someone we met:

Best story told:

The kids liked this:

The best food:

Games played:

Something disappointing:

Next time I'll do this differently:

Stone Mountain State Park
City: Roaring Gap   County: Alleghany
Plan your trip: https://www.ncparks.gov/stone-mountain-state-park/home

Activities:

- ❏ Biking
- ❏ Boating
- ❏ Disc Golf
- ❏ Fishing
- ❏ Gold Panning
- ❏ Hiking
- ❏ Historic Learning
- ❏ Horseback Riding
- ❏ Hunting
- ❏ Kite Boarding

- ❏ Metal Detecting
- ❏ OHV
- ❏ Paddling
- ❏ Rock Climbing
- ❏ Stargazing
- ❏ Swimming
- ❏ Wildlife Viewing
- ❏ Windsurfing
- ❏
- ❏

- ❏
- ❏
- ❏
- ❏
- ❏
- ❏
- ❏
- ❏
- ❏
- ❏

Get the Facts

- ❏ Phone   336-957-8185
- ❏ Park Hours

  _____

- ❏ Reservations? ____Y ____N

  date made_____
- ❏ Open all year ____Y____N

  dates_____
- ❏ Check in time _____
- ❏ Check out time _____
- ❏ Pet friendly _____Y _____N
- ❏ Max RV length _____
- ❏ Distance from home

  miles: _____

  hours: _____
- ❏ Address_____

  _____

  _____

Facilities:

- ❏ ADA
- ❏ Picnic sites
- ❏ Restrooms
- ❏ Showers
- ❏ Trailer Access
- ❏ Visitor center
- ❏ Group Camping
- ❏ RV Camp
- ❏ Rustic Camping
- ❏ Cabins / Yurts
- ❏ Day Use Area

Notes:

Fees:

- ❏ Day Use $ _____
- ❏ Camp Sites $ _____
- ❏ RV Sites $ _____
- ❏ Refund policy

  _____

  _____

  _____

Make It Personal

Trip dates:

The weather was: Sunny Cloudy Rainy Stormy Snowy Foggy Warm Cold

Why I went:

How I got there: (circle all that apply) Plane   Train   Car   Bus   Bike   Hike   RV   MC

I went with:

We stayed in (space, cabin # etc):

Most relaxing day:

Something funny:

Someone we met:

Best story told:

The kids liked this:

The best food:

Games played:

Something disappointing:

Next time I'll do this differently:

43

Grandfather Mountain State Park
City: Banner Elk   County: Avery

Plan your trip: https://www.ncparks.gov/grandfather-mountain-state-park/home

Activities:

- ☐ Biking
- ☐ Boating
- ☐ Disc Golf
- ☐ Fishing
- ☐ Gold Panning
- ☐ Hiking
- ☐ Historic Learning
- ☐ Horseback Riding
- ☐ Hunting
- ☐ Kite Boarding

- ☐ Metal Detecting
- ☐ OHV
- ☐ Paddling
- ☐ Rock Climbing
- ☐ Stargazing
- ☐ Swimming
- ☐ Wildlife Viewing
- ☐ Windsurfing
- ☐
- ☐

- ☐
- ☐
- ☐
- ☐
- ☐
- ☐
- ☐
- ☐
- ☐
- ☐

Facilities:

- ☐ ADA
- ☐ Picnic sites
- ☐ Restrooms
- ☐ Showers
- ☐ Trailer Access
- ☐ Visitor center
- ☐ Group Camping
- ☐ RV Camp
- ☐ Rustic Camping
- ☐ Cabins / Yurts
- ☐ Day Use Area

Notes:

Get the Facts

- ☐ Phone   828-963-9522
- ☐ Park Hours

  _____

- ☐ Reservations? ____Y ____N

  date made_____
- ☐ Open all year ____Y____N

  dates_____
- ☐ Check in time _____
- ☐ Check out time _____
- ☐ Pet friendly _____Y _____N
- ☐ Max RV length _____
- ☐ Distance from home

  miles: _____

  hours: _____
- ☐ Address_____

  _____

  _____

Fees:

- ☐ Day Use $ _____
- ☐ Camp Sites $ _____
- ☐ RV Sites $ _____
- ☐ Refund policy

  _____

  _____

  _____

Make It Personal

Trip dates: | The weather was: Sunny Cloudy Rainy Stormy Snowy Foggy Warm Cold

Why I went:

How I got there: (circle all that apply)   Plane   Train   Car   Bus   Bike   Hike   RV   MC

I went with:

We stayed in (space, cabin # etc):

Most relaxing day:

Something funny:

Someone we met:

Best story told:

The kids liked this:

The best food:

Games played:

Something disappointing:

Next time I'll do this differently:

Biltmore Estate
City: Asheville   County: Buncombe

Plan your trip: https://www.biltmore.com/

Activities:

- ☐ Biking
- ☐ Boating
- ☐ Disc Golf
- ☐ Fishing
- ☐ Gold Panning
- ☐ Hiking
- ☐ Historic Learning
- ☐ Horseback Riding
- ☐ Hunting
- ☐ Kite Boarding
- ☐ Metal Detecting
- ☐ OHV
- ☐ Paddling
- ☐ Rock Climbing
- ☐ Stargazing
- ☐ Swimming
- ☐ Wildlife Viewing
- ☐ Windsurfing
- ☐
- ☐
- ☐
- ☐
- ☐
- ☐
- ☐
- ☐
- ☐
- ☐
- ☐
- ☐
- ☐

Facilities:

- ☐ ADA
- ☐ Picnic sites
- ☐ Restrooms
- ☐ Showers
- ☐ Trailer Access
- ☐ Visitor center
- ☐ Group Camping
- ☐ RV Camp
- ☐ Rustic Camping
- ☐ Cabins / Yurts
- ☐ Day Use Area

Notes:

Get the Facts

- ☐ Phone   800-411-3812
- ☐ Park Hours

_____

- ☐ Reservations? ____Y ____N

date made_____

- ☐ Open all year ____Y____N

dates_____

- ☐ Check in time _____
- ☐ Check out time _____
- ☐ Pet friendly _____Y _____N
- ☐ Max RV length _____
- ☐ Distance from home

miles: _____

hours: _____

- ☐ Address_____

_____

_____

Fees:

- ☐ Day Use $ _____
- ☐ Camp Sites $ _____
- ☐ RV Sites $ _____
- ☐ Refund policy

_____

_____

_____

Make It Personal

Trip dates: | The weather was: Sunny Cloudy Rainy Stormy Snowy Foggy Warm Cold

Why I went:

How I got there: (circle all that apply) Plane Train Car Bus Bike Hike RV MC

I went with:

We stayed in (space, cabin # etc):

Most relaxing day:

Something funny:

Someone we met:

Best story told:

The kids liked this:

The best food:

Games played:

Something disappointing:

Next time I'll do this differently:

South Mountains State Park
City: Connelly Springs   County: Burke

Plan your trip: https://www.ncparks.gov/south-mountains-state-park/home

Activities:

- ❏ Biking
- ❏ Boating
- ❏ Disc Golf
- ❏ Fishing
- ❏ Gold Panning
- ❏ Hiking
- ❏ Historic Learning
- ❏ Horseback Riding
- ❏ Hunting
- ❏ Kite Boarding

- ❏ Metal Detecting
- ❏ OHV
- ❏ Paddling
- ❏ Rock Climbing
- ❏ Stargazing
- ❏ Swimming
- ❏ Wildlife Viewing
- ❏ Windsurfing
- ❏
- ❏

- ❏
- ❏
- ❏
- ❏
- ❏
- ❏
- ❏
- ❏
- ❏
- ❏

Facilities:

- ❏ ADA
- ❏ Picnic sites
- ❏ Restrooms
- ❏ Showers
- ❏ Trailer Access
- ❏ Visitor center
- ❏ Group Camping
- ❏ RV Camp
- ❏ Rustic Camping
- ❏ Cabins / Yurts
- ❏ Day Use Area

Notes:

Get the Facts

- ❏ Phone   828-433-4772
- ❏ Park Hours

  _____

- ❏ Reservations? ____Y ____N

  date made_____
- ❏ Open all year ____Y_____N

  dates_____
- ❏ Check in time _____
- ❏ Check out time _____
- ❏ Pet friendly _____Y _____N
- ❏ Max RV length _____
- ❏ Distance from home

  miles: _____

  hours: _____
- ❏ Address_____

  _____

  _____

Fees:

- ❏ Day Use $ _____
- ❏ Camp Sites $ _____
- ❏ RV Sites $ _____
- ❏ Refund policy

  _____

  _____

  _____

Make It Personal

Trip dates:

The weather was: Sunny Cloudy Rainy Stormy Snowy Foggy Warm Cold

Why I went:

How I got there: (circle all that apply) Plane Train Car Bus Bike Hike RV MC

I went with:

We stayed in (space, cabin # etc):

Most relaxing day:

Something funny:

Someone we met:

Best story told:

The kids liked this:

The best food:

Games played:

Something disappointing:

Next time I'll do this differently:

Lake James State Park
City: Nebo   County: McDowell
Plan your trip: https://www.ncparks.gov/lake-james-state-park/home

Activities:

- ❑ Biking
- ❑ Boating
- ❑ Disc Golf
- ❑ Fishing
- ❑ Gold Panning
- ❑ Hiking
- ❑ Historic Learning
- ❑ Horseback Riding
- ❑ Hunting
- ❑ Kite Boarding

- ❑ Metal Detecting
- ❑ OHV
- ❑ Paddling
- ❑ Rock Climbing
- ❑ Stargazing
- ❑ Swimming
- ❑ Wildlife Viewing
- ❑ Windsurfing
- ❑
- ❑

- ❑
- ❑
- ❑
- ❑
- ❑
- ❑
- ❑
- ❑
- ❑
- ❑

Facilities:

- ❑ ADA
- ❑ Picnic sites
- ❑ Restrooms
- ❑ Showers
- ❑ Trailer Access
- ❑ Visitor center
- ❑ Group Camping
- ❑ RV Camp
- ❑ Rustic Camping
- ❑ Cabins / Yurts
- ❑ Day Use Area

Notes:

Get the Facts

- ❑ Phone   828-584-7728
- ❑ Park Hours

  _____

- ❑ Reservations? ____Y ____N

  date made_____

- ❑ Open all year ____Y____N

  dates_____

- ❑ Check in time _____

- ❑ Check out time _____

- ❑ Pet friendly _____Y _____N

- ❑ Max RV length _____

- ❑ Distance from home

  miles: _____

  hours: _____

- ❑ Address_____

  _____

  _____

Fees:

- ❑ Day Use $ _____
- ❑ Camp Sites $ _____
- ❑ RV Sites $ _____
- ❑ Refund policy

  _____

  _____

  _____

Make It Personal

Trip dates:

The weather was: Sunny Cloudy Rainy Stormy Snowy Foggy Warm Cold

Why I went:

How I got there: (circle all that apply) Plane Train Car Bus Bike Hike RV MC

I went with:

We stayed in (space, cabin # etc):

Most relaxing day:

Something funny:

Someone we met:

Best story told:

The kids liked this:

The best food:

Games played:

Something disappointing:

Next time I'll do this differently:

Gorges State Park
City: Sapphire
County: Transylvania

Plan your trip: https://www.ncparks.gov/gorges-state-park/home

Activities:

- ❑ Biking
- ❑ Boating
- ❑ Disc Golf
- ❑ Fishing
- ❑ Gold Panning
- ❑ Hiking
- ❑ Historic Learning
- ❑ Horseback Riding
- ❑ Hunting
- ❑ Kite Boarding

- ❑ Metal Detecting
- ❑ OHV
- ❑ Paddling
- ❑ Rock Climbing
- ❑ Stargazing
- ❑ Swimming
- ❑ Wildlife Viewing
- ❑ Windsurfing
- ❑
- ❑

- ❑
- ❑
- ❑
- ❑
- ❑
- ❑
- ❑
- ❑
- ❑
- ❑

Facilities:

- ❑ ADA
- ❑ Picnic sites
- ❑ Restrooms
- ❑ Showers
- ❑ Trailer Access
- ❑ Visitor center
- ❑ Group Camping
- ❑ RV Camp
- ❑ Rustic Camping
- ❑ Cabins / Yurts
- ❑ Day Use Area

Notes:

Get the Facts

- ❑ Phone   828-966-9099
- ❑ Park Hours

  _____

- ❑ Reservations? _____Y _____N

  date made_____

- ❑ Open all year _____Y_____N

  dates_____

- ❑ Check in time _____

- ❑ Check out time _____

- ❑ Pet friendly _____Y _____N

- ❑ Max RV length _____

- ❑ Distance from home

  miles: _____

  hours: _____

- ❑ Address_____

  _____

  _____

Fees:

- ❑ Day Use $ _____
- ❑ Camp Sites $ _____
- ❑ RV Sites $ _____
- ❑ Refund policy

  _____

  _____

  _____

Make It Personal

Trip dates: | The weather was: Sunny Cloudy Rainy Stormy Snowy Foggy Warm Cold

Why I went:

How I got there: (circle all that apply)   Plane   Train   Car   Bus   Bike   Hike   RV   MC

I went with:

We stayed in (space, cabin # etc):

Most relaxing day:

Something funny:

Someone we met:

Best story told:

The kids liked this:

The best food:

Games played:

Something disappointing:

Next time I'll do this differently:

Julian Price Memorial Park
City: Blowing Rock   County: Watauga
Plan your trip: https://www.ncparks.gov/mount-mitchell-state-park/home/

Activities:

- ❑ Biking
- ❑ Boating
- ❑ Disc Golf
- ❑ Fishing
- ❑ Gold Panning
- ❑ Hiking
- ❑ Historic Learning
- ❑ Horseback Riding
- ❑ Hunting
- ❑ Kite Boarding

- ❑ Metal Detecting
- ❑ OHV
- ❑ Paddling
- ❑ Rock Climbing
- ❑ Stargazing
- ❑ Swimming
- ❑ Wildlife Viewing
- ❑ Windsurfing
- ❑
- ❑

- ❑
- ❑
- ❑
- ❑
- ❑
- ❑
- ❑
- ❑
- ❑
- ❑

Facilities:

- ❑ ADA
- ❑ Picnic sites
- ❑ Restrooms
- ❑ Showers
- ❑ Trailer Access
- ❑ Visitor center
- ❑ Group Camping
- ❑ RV Camp
- ❑ Rustic Camping
- ❑ Cabins / Yurts
- ❑ Day Use Area

Notes:

Get the Facts

- ❑ Phone   828-295-7591
- ❑ Park Hours

  _____

- ❑ Reservations? _____Y _____N

  date made_____

- ❑ Open all year _____Y_____N

  dates_____

- ❑ Check in time _____
- ❑ Check out time _____
- ❑ Pet friendly _____Y _____N
- ❑ Max RV length _____
- ❑ Distance from home

  miles: _____

  hours: _____

- ❑ Address_____

  _____

  _____

Fees:

- ❑ Day Use $ _____
- ❑ Camp Sites $ _____
- ❑ RV Sites $ _____
- ❑ Refund policy

  _____

  _____

  _____

Make It Personal

Trip dates: _____

The weather was: Sunny Cloudy Rainy Stormy Snowy Foggy Warm Cold

Why I went: _____

How I got there: (circle all that apply) Plane Train Car Bus Bike Hike RV MC

I went with: _____

We stayed in (space, cabin # etc): _____

Most relaxing day: _____

Something funny: _____

Someone we met: _____

Best story told: _____

The kids liked this: _____

The best food: _____

Games played: _____

Something disappointing: _____

Next time I'll do this differently: _____

Mount Mitchell State Park
City: Burnsville   County: Yancey
Plan your trip: https://www.ncparks.gov/mount-mitchell-state-park/home

Activities:

- ❑ Biking
- ❑ Boating
- ❑ Disc Golf
- ❑ Fishing
- ❑ Gold Panning
- ❑ Hiking
- ❑ Historic Learning
- ❑ Horseback Riding
- ❑ Hunting
- ❑ Kite Boarding

- ❑ Metal Detecting
- ❑ OHV
- ❑ Paddling
- ❑ Rock Climbing
- ❑ Stargazing
- ❑ Swimming
- ❑ Wildlife Viewing
- ❑ Windsurfing
- ❑
- ❑

- ❑
- ❑
- ❑
- ❑
- ❑
- ❑
- ❑
- ❑
- ❑
- ❑

Facilities:

- ❑ ADA
- ❑ Picnic sites
- ❑ Restrooms
- ❑ Showers
- ❑ Trailer Access
- ❑ Visitor center
- ❑ Group Camping
- ❑ RV Camp
- ❑ Rustic Camping
- ❑ Cabins / Yurts
- ❑ Day Use Area

Notes:

Get the Facts

- ❑ Phone   828-675-4611
- ❑ Park Hours

  _____

- ❑ Reservations? ____Y ____N

  date made_____
- ❑ Open all year ____Y____N

  dates_____
- ❑ Check in time _____
- ❑ Check out time _____
- ❑ Pet friendly _____Y _____N
- ❑ Max RV length _____
- ❑ Distance from home

  miles: _____

  hours: _____
- ❑ Address_____

  _____

  _____

Fees:

- ❑ Day Use $ _____
- ❑ Camp Sites $ _____
- ❑ RV Sites $ _____
- ❑ Refund policy

  _____

  _____

  _____

Make It Personal

Trip dates: _____

The weather was: Sunny Cloudy Rainy Stormy Snowy Foggy Warm Cold

_____

Why I went:

_____

_____

How I got there: (circle all that apply)   Plane   Train   Car   Bus   Bike   Hike   RV   MC

_____

I went with:

_____

We stayed in (space, cabin # etc):

_____

Most relaxing day:

_____

_____

Something funny:

_____

_____

Someone we met:

_____

_____

Best story told:

_____

_____

The kids liked this:

_____

_____

The best food:

_____

_____

Games played:

_____

_____

Something disappointing:

_____

_____

Next time I'll do this differently:

_____

_____

57

Elk Knob State Park
City: Todd　　　　　　　County: Ashe
Plan your trip: https://www.ncparks.gov/elk-knob-state-park/home

Activities:

- ❑ ATV / OHV　　　❑
- ❑ Bike Trails　　　❑
- ❑ Birding　　　　❑
- ❑ Boating　　　　❑
- ❑ Fishing　　　　❑
- ❑ Hiking　　　　❑
- ❑ Horseback　　　❑
- ❑ Mountain Biking　❑
- ❑ Watersports　　❑
- ❑ Wildlife　　　　❑
- ❑ Winter Sports

Facilities:

- ❑ ADA　　　　　❑
- ❑ Gift Shop　　　❑
- ❑ Museum　　　　❑
- ❑ Visitor Center　❑
- ❑ Picnic sites　　❑
- ❑ Restrooms　　　❑

Things to do in the area:

Get the Facts

- ❑ Phone 252-771-6593
- ❑ Park Hours

  _____

- ❑ Reservations? _____Y _____N

  date made_____

- ❑ Open all year? _____Y_____N

  dates_____

- ❑ Dog friendly _____Y _____N

- ❑ Distance from home

  miles: _____

  hours: _____

- ❑ Address_____

  _____

  _____

Fees:

- ❑ Day Use $ _____
- ❑ Refund policy

  _____

  _____

  _____

Notes:

Mount Jefferson State Natural Area
City: West Jefferson   County: Ashe

Plan your trip: https://www.ncparks.gov/mount-jefferson-state-natural-area/home

Activities:

- ❏ ATV / OHV   ❏
- ❏ Bike Trails   ❏
- ❏ Birding   ❏
- ❏ Boating   ❏
- ❏ Fishing   ❏
- ❏ Hiking   ❏
- ❏ Horseback   ❏
- ❏ Mountain Biking   ❏
- ❏ Watersports   ❏
- ❏ Wildlife   ❏
- ❏ Winter Sports

Facilities:

- ❏ ADA   ❏
- ❏ Gift Shop   ❏
- ❏ Museum   ❏
- ❏ Visitor Center   ❏
- ❏ Picnic sites   ❏
- ❏ Restrooms   ❏

Things to do in the area:

Get the Facts

- ❏ Phone 336-246-9653
- ❏ Park Hours

  _____

- ❏ Reservations? _____Y _____N

  date made_____

- ❏ Open all year? _____Y_____N

  dates_____

- ❏ Dog friendly _____Y _____N

- ❏ Distance from home

  miles: _____

  hours: _____

- ❏ Address_____

  _____

  _____

Fees:

- ❏ Day Use $ _____
- ❏ Refund policy

  _____

  _____

  _____

Notes:

Thomas Wolfe Memorial Historic Site

City: Asheville   **County: Buncombe**

Plan your trip: https://historicsites.nc.gov/node/68

Activities:

- [ ] ATV / OHV   [ ]
- [ ] Bike Trails   [ ]
- [ ] Birding   [ ]
- [ ] Boating   [ ]
- [ ] Fishing   [ ]
- [ ] Hiking   [ ]
- [ ] Horseback   [ ]
- [ ] Mountain Biking   [ ]
- [ ] Watersports   [ ]
- [ ] Wildlife   [ ]
- [ ] Winter Sports

Facilities:

- [ ] ADA   [ ]
- [ ] Gift Shop   [ ]
- [ ] Museum   [ ]
- [ ] Visitor Center   [ ]
- [ ] Picnic sites   [ ]
- [ ] Restrooms   [ ]

Things to do in the area:

Get the Facts

- [ ] Phone 828-253-8304
- [ ] Park Hours

  _____

- [ ] Reservations? _____Y _____N

  date made_____

- [ ] Open all year? _____Y_____N

  dates_____

- [ ] Dog friendly _____Y _____N

- [ ] Distance from home

  miles: _____

  hours: _____

- [ ] Address_____

  _____

  _____

Fees:

- [ ] Day Use $ _____
- [ ] Refund policy

  _____

  _____

  _____

Notes:

Zebulon B. Vance Birthplace Historic Site
City: Weaverville   County: Buncombe

Plan your trip: https://historicsites.nc.gov/node/70

Activities:

- ❑ ATV / OHV   ❑
- ❑ Bike Trails   ❑
- ❑ Birding   ❑
- ❑ Boating   ❑
- ❑ Fishing   ❑
- ❑ Hiking   ❑
- ❑ Horseback   ❑
- ❑ Mountain Biking   ❑
- ❑ Watersports   ❑
- ❑ Wildlife   ❑
- ❑ Winter Sports

Facilities:

- ❑ ADA   ❑
- ❑ Gift Shop   ❑
- ❑ Museum   ❑
- ❑ Visitor Center   ❑
- ❑ Picnic sites   ❑
- ❑ Restrooms   ❑

Things to do in the area:

Get the Facts

- ❑ Phone 828-645-6706
- ❑ Park Hours

  _____

- ❑ Reservations? ____Y ____N

  date made_____

- ❑ Open all year? ____Y____N

  dates_____

- ❑ Dog friendly ____Y ____N

- ❑ Distance from home

  miles: _____

  hours: _____

- ❑ Address_____

  _____

  _____

Fees:

- ❑ Day Use $ _____
- ❑ Refund policy

  _____

  _____

  _____

Notes:

Chimney Rock State Park
City: Chimney Rock   County: Rutherford

Plan your trip: https://www.ncparks.gov/chimney-rock-state-park/home

Activities:

- ❑ ATV / OHV   ❑
- ❑ Bike Trails   ❑
- ❑ Birding   ❑
- ❑ Boating   ❑
- ❑ Fishing   ❑
- ❑ Hiking   ❑
- ❑ Horseback   ❑
- ❑ Mountain Biking   ❑
- ❑ Watersports   ❑
- ❑ Wildlife   ❑
- ❑ Winter Sports

Facilities:

- ❑ ADA   ❑
- ❑ Gift Shop   ❑
- ❑ Museum   ❑
- ❑ Visitor Center   ❑
- ❑ Picnic sites   ❑
- ❑ Restrooms   ❑

Things to do in the area:

Get the Facts

- ❑ Phone 828-625-1823
- ❑ Park Hours

  _____

- ❑ Reservations? _____Y _____N

  date made_____

- ❑ Open all year? _____Y_____N

  dates_____

- ❑ Dog friendly _____Y _____N

- ❑ Distance from home

  miles: _____

  hours: _____

- ❑ Address_____

  _____

  _____

Fees:

- ❑ Day Use $ _____
- ❑ Refund policy

  _____

  _____

  _____

Notes:

Moses H Cone Memorial Park
City: Blowing Rock   County: Watauga

Plan your trip: https://www.blueridgeheritage.com/destinations/moses-cone-manor/

Activities:

- ❑ ATV / OHV   ❑
- ❑ Bike Trails   ❑
- ❑ Birding   ❑
- ❑ Boating   ❑
- ❑ Fishing   ❑
- ❑ Hiking   ❑
- ❑ Horseback   ❑
- ❑ Mountain Biking   ❑
- ❑ Watersports   ❑
- ❑ Wildlife   ❑
- ❑ Winter Sports

Facilities:

- ❑ ADA   ❑
- ❑ Gift Shop   ❑
- ❑ Museum   ❑
- ❑ Visitor Center   ❑
- ❑ Picnic sites   ❑
- ❑ Restrooms   ❑

Things to do in the area:

Get the Facts

- ❑ Phone 828-295-3782
- ❑ Park Hours

  _____

- ❑ Reservations? ____Y ____N

  date made_____

- ❑ Open all year? ____Y____N

  dates_____

- ❑ Dog friendly _____Y _____N

- ❑ Distance from home

  miles: _____

  hours: _____

- ❑ Address_____

  _____

  _____

Fees:

- ❑ Day Use $ _____
- ❑ Refund policy

  _____

  _____

  _____

Notes:

Rendezvous Mountain Educational State Forest

City: Rendezvous   County: Wilkes

Plan your trip: https://www.ncesf.org/rendezvousMt.html

Activities:

- ☐ ATV / OHV   ☐
- ☐ Bike Trails   ☐
- ☐ Birding   ☐
- ☐ Boating   ☐
- ☐ Fishing   ☐
- ☐ Hiking   ☐
- ☐ Horseback   ☐
- ☐ Mountain Biking   ☐
- ☐ Watersports   ☐
- ☐ Wildlife   ☐
- ☐ Winter Sports

Facilities:

- ☐ ADA   ☐
- ☐ Gift Shop   ☐
- ☐ Museum   ☐
- ☐ Visitor Center   ☐
- ☐ Picnic sites   ☐
- ☐ Restrooms   ☐

Things to do in the area:

Get the Facts

- ☐ Phone   336-667-5072
- ☐ Park Hours

  _____

- ☐ Reservations? ____Y ____N

  date made_____

- ☐ Open all year? ____Y____N

  dates_____

- ☐ Dog friendly _____Y _____N

- ☐ Distance from home

  miles: _____

  hours: _____

- ☐ Address_____

  _____

  _____

Fees:

- ☐ Day Use $ _____
- ☐ Refund policy

  _____

  _____

  _____

Notes:

Crowders Mountain State Park
City: Kings Mountain   County: Cleveland
Plan your trip: https://www.ncparks.gov/crowders-mountain-state-park/activities

Activities:

- ❑ Biking
- ❑ Boating
- ❑ Disc Golf
- ❑ Fishing
- ❑ Gold Panning
- ❑ Hiking
- ❑ Historic Learning
- ❑ Horseback Riding
- ❑ Hunting
- ❑ Kite Boarding
- ❑ Metal Detecting
- ❑ OHV
- ❑ Paddling
- ❑ Rock Climbing
- ❑ Stargazing
- ❑ Swimming
- ❑ Wildlife Viewing
- ❑ Windsurfing
- ❑
- ❑
- ❑
- ❑
- ❑
- ❑
- ❑
- ❑
- ❑
- ❑
- ❑
- ❑

Facilities:

- ❑ ADA
- ❑ Picnic sites
- ❑ Restrooms
- ❑ Showers
- ❑ Trailer Access
- ❑ Visitor center
- ❑ Group Camping
- ❑ RV Camp
- ❑ Rustic Camping
- ❑ Cabins / Yurts
- ❑ Day Use Area

Notes:

Get the Facts

- ❑ Phone   704-853-5375
- ❑ Park Hours

  _____

- ❑ Reservations? ____Y ____N

  date made_____
- ❑ Open all year ____Y____N

  dates_____
- ❑ Check in time _____
- ❑ Check out time _____
- ❑ Pet friendly _____Y _____N
- ❑ Max RV length _____
- ❑ Distance from home

  miles: _____

  hours: _____
- ❑ Address_____

  _____

  _____

Fees:

- ❑ Day Use $ _____
- ❑ Camp Sites $ _____
- ❑ RV Sites $ _____
- ❑ Refund policy

  _____

  _____

  _____

Make It Personal

Trip dates:

The weather was: Sunny Cloudy Rainy Stormy Snowy Foggy Warm Cold

Why I went:

How I got there: (circle all that apply) Plane Train Car Bus Bike Hike RV MC

I went with:

We stayed in (space, cabin # etc):

Most relaxing day:

Something funny:

Someone we met:

Best story told:

The kids liked this:

The best food:

Games played:

Something disappointing:

Next time I'll do this differently:

Hanging Rock State Park
City: Danbury   County: Stokes
Plan your trip: https://www.ncparks.gov/hanging-rock-state-park/home

Activities:

- ❑ Biking
- ❑ Boating
- ❑ Disc Golf
- ❑ Fishing
- ❑ Gold Panning
- ❑ Hiking
- ❑ Historic Learning
- ❑ Horseback Riding
- ❑ Hunting
- ❑ Kite Boarding
- ❑ Metal Detecting
- ❑ OHV
- ❑ Paddling
- ❑ Rock Climbing
- ❑ Stargazing
- ❑ Swimming
- ❑ Wildlife Viewing
- ❑ Windsurfing

Facilities:

- ❑ ADA
- ❑ Picnic sites
- ❑ Restrooms
- ❑ Showers
- ❑ Trailer Access
- ❑ Visitor center
- ❑ Group Camping
- ❑ RV Camp
- ❑ Rustic Camping
- ❑ Cabins / Yurts
- ❑ Day Use Area

Notes:

Get the Facts

- ❑ Phone   336-593-8480
- ❑ Park Hours

  _____
- ❑ Reservations? ____Y ____N

  date made_____
- ❑ Open all year ____Y____N

  dates_____
- ❑ Check in time _____
- ❑ Check out time _____
- ❑ Pet friendly _____Y _____N
- ❑ Max RV length _____
- ❑ Distance from home

  miles: _____

  hours: _____
- ❑ Address_____

  _____

  _____

Fees:

- ❑ Day Use $ _____
- ❑ Camp Sites $ _____
- ❑ RV Sites $ _____
- ❑ Refund policy

  _____

  _____

  _____

Make It Personal

Trip dates: | The weather was: Sunny Cloudy Rainy Stormy Snowy Foggy Warm Cold

Why I went:

How I got there: (circle all that apply) Plane Train Car Bus Bike Hike RV MC

I went with:

We stayed in (space, cabin # etc):

Most relaxing day:

Something funny:

Someone we met:

Best story told:

The kids liked this:

The best food:

Games played:

Something disappointing:

Next time I'll do this differently:

Boones Cave Park
City: Lexington   County: Davidson
Plan your trip: https://www.co.davidson.nc.us/Facilities/Facility/Details/Boones-Cave-Park-10

Activities:

- ❑ Biking
- ❑ Boating
- ❑ Disc Golf
- ❑ Fishing
- ❑ Gold Panning
- ❑ Hiking
- ❑ Historic Learning
- ❑ Horseback Riding
- ❑ Hunting
- ❑ Kite Boarding

- ❑ Metal Detecting
- ❑ OHV
- ❑ Paddling
- ❑ Rock Climbing
- ❑ Stargazing
- ❑ Swimming
- ❑ Wildlife Viewing
- ❑ Windsurfing
- ❑
- ❑

- ❑
- ❑
- ❑
- ❑
- ❑
- ❑
- ❑
- ❑
- ❑
- ❑

Facilities:

- ❑ ADA
- ❑ Picnic sites
- ❑ Restrooms
- ❑ Showers
- ❑ Trailer Access
- ❑ Visitor center
- ❑ Group Camping
- ❑ RV Camp
- ❑ Rustic Camping
- ❑ Cabins / Yurts
- ❑ Day Use Area

Notes:

Get the Facts

- ❑ Phone   336-752-2322
- ❑ Park Hours

   _____

- ❑ Reservations? ____Y ____N

   date made_____
- ❑ Open all year ____Y____N

   dates_____
- ❑ Check in time _____
- ❑ Check out time _____
- ❑ Pet friendly _____Y _____N
- ❑ Max RV length _____
- ❑ Distance from home

   miles: _____

   hours: _____
- ❑ Address_____

   _____

   _____

Fees:

- ❑ Day Use $ _____
- ❑ Camp Sites $ _____
- ❑ RV Sites $ _____
- ❑ Refund policy

   _____

   _____

   _____

Make It Personal

Trip dates:

The weather was: Sunny Cloudy Rainy Stormy Snowy Foggy Warm Cold

Why I went:

How I got there: (circle all that apply) Plane Train Car Bus Bike Hike RV MC

I went with:

We stayed in (space, cabin # etc):

Most relaxing day:

Something funny:

Someone we met:

Best story told:

The kids liked this:

The best food:

Games played:

Something disappointing:

Next time I'll do this differently:

Eno River State Park
City: Durham   County: Durham
Plan your trip: https://www.ncparks.gov/eno-river-state-park/home

Activities:

- ❑ Biking
- ❑ Boating
- ❑ Disc Golf
- ❑ Fishing
- ❑ Gold Panning
- ❑ Hiking
- ❑ Historic Learning
- ❑ Horseback Riding
- ❑ Hunting
- ❑ Kite Boarding

- ❑ Metal Detecting
- ❑ OHV
- ❑ Paddling
- ❑ Rock Climbing
- ❑ Stargazing
- ❑ Swimming
- ❑ Wildlife Viewing
- ❑ Windsurfing
- ❑
- ❑

- ❑
- ❑
- ❑
- ❑
- ❑
- ❑
- ❑
- ❑
- ❑
- ❑

Facilities:

- ❑ ADA
- ❑ Picnic sites
- ❑ Restrooms
- ❑ Showers
- ❑ Trailer Access
- ❑ Visitor center
- ❑ Group Camping
- ❑ RV Camp
- ❑ Rustic Camping
- ❑ Cabins / Yurts
- ❑ Day Use Area

Notes:

Get the Facts

- ❑ Phone   919-383-1686
- ❑ Park Hours

  _____

- ❑ Reservations? ____Y ____N

  date made_____
- ❑ Open all year ____Y_____N

  dates_____
- ❑ Check in time _____
- ❑ Check out time _____
- ❑ Pet friendly _____Y _____N
- ❑ Max RV length _____
- ❑ Distance from home

  miles: _____

  hours: _____
- ❑ Address_____

  _____

  _____

Fees:

- ❑ Day Use $ _____
- ❑ Camp Sites $ _____
- ❑ RV Sites $ _____
- ❑ Refund policy

  _____

  _____

  _____

Make It Personal

Trip dates: _____

The weather was: Sunny Cloudy Rainy Stormy Snowy Foggy Warm Cold

Why I went:

_____

_____

How I got there: (circle all that apply) Plane Train Car Bus Bike Hike RV MC

I went with:

_____

We stayed in (space, cabin # etc):

_____

Most relaxing day:

_____

_____

Something funny:

_____

_____

Someone we met:

_____

_____

Best story told:

_____

_____

The kids liked this:

_____

_____

The best food:

_____

_____

Games played:

_____

_____

Something disappointing:

_____

_____

Next time I'll do this differently:

_____

_____

Little River Regional Park & Natural Area

City: Rougemont   County: Durham

Plan your trip: http://www.orangecountync.gov/Facilities/Facility/Details/Little-River-Regional-Park-Natural-Area-7

Activities:

- ❑ Biking
- ❑ Boating
- ❑ Disc Golf
- ❑ Fishing
- ❑ Gold Panning
- ❑ Hiking
- ❑ Historic Learning
- ❑ Horseback Riding
- ❑ Hunting
- ❑ Kite Boarding

- ❑ Metal Detecting
- ❑ OHV
- ❑ Paddling
- ❑ Rock Climbing
- ❑ Stargazing
- ❑ Swimming
- ❑ Wildlife Viewing
- ❑ Windsurfing
- ❑
- ❑

- ❑
- ❑
- ❑
- ❑
- ❑
- ❑
- ❑
- ❑
- ❑
- ❑
- ❑

Facilities:

- ❑ ADA
- ❑ Picnic sites
- ❑ Restrooms
- ❑ Showers
- ❑ Trailer Access
- ❑ Visitor center
- ❑ Group Camping
- ❑ RV Camp
- ❑ Rustic Camping
- ❑ Cabins / Yurts
- ❑ Day Use Area

Notes:

Get the Facts

- ❑ Phone   919-732-5505
- ❑ Park Hours

    _____

- ❑ Reservations? _____Y _____N

    date made_____

- ❑ Open all year _____Y_____N

    dates_____

- ❑ Check in time _____
- ❑ Check out time _____
- ❑ Pet friendly _____Y _____N
- ❑ Max RV length _____
- ❑ Distance from home

    miles: _____

    hours: _____

- ❑ Address_____

    _____

    _____

Fees:

- ❑ Day Use $ _____
- ❑ Camp Sites $ _____
- ❑ RV Sites $ _____
- ❑ Refund policy

    _____

    _____

    _____

Make It Personal

Trip dates:

The weather was: Sunny Cloudy Rainy Stormy Snowy Foggy Warm Cold

Why I went:

How I got there: (circle all that apply) Plane Train Car Bus Bike Hike RV MC

I went with:

We stayed in (space, cabin # etc):

Most relaxing day:

Something funny:

Someone we met:

Best story told:

The kids liked this:

The best food:

Games played:

Something disappointing:

Next time I'll do this differently:

Haw River State Park
City: Browns Summit   County: Guilford
Plan your trip: https://www.ncparks.gov/haw-river-state-park/home

Activities:

- [ ] Biking
- [ ] Boating
- [ ] Disc Golf
- [ ] Fishing
- [ ] Gold Panning
- [ ] Hiking
- [ ] Historic Learning
- [ ] Horseback Riding
- [ ] Hunting
- [ ] Kite Boarding
- [ ] Metal Detecting
- [ ] OHV
- [ ] Paddling
- [ ] Rock Climbing
- [ ] Stargazing
- [ ] Swimming
- [ ] Wildlife Viewing
- [ ] Windsurfing
- [ ]
- [ ]
- [ ]
- [ ]
- [ ]
- [ ]
- [ ]
- [ ]
- [ ]
- [ ]
- [ ]
- [ ]

Facilities:

- [ ] ADA
- [ ] Picnic sites
- [ ] Restrooms
- [ ] Showers
- [ ] Trailer Access
- [ ] Visitor center
- [ ] Group Camping
- [ ] RV Camp
- [ ] Rustic Camping
- [ ] Cabins / Yurts
- [ ] Day Use Area

Notes:

Get the Facts

- [ ] Phone   336-342-6163
- [ ] Park Hours

  _____

- [ ] Reservations? ____Y ____N

  date made_____
- [ ] Open all year ____Y_____N

  dates_____
- [ ] Check in time _____
- [ ] Check out time _____
- [ ] Pet friendly _____Y _____N
- [ ] Max RV length _____
- [ ] Distance from home

  miles: _____

  hours: _____
- [ ] Address_____

  _____

  _____

Fees:

- [ ] Day Use $ _____
- [ ] Camp Sites $ _____
- [ ] RV Sites $ _____
- [ ] Refund policy

  _____

  _____

  _____

Make It Personal

Trip dates:

The weather was: Sunny Cloudy Rainy Stormy Snowy Foggy Warm Cold

Why I went:

How I got there: (circle all that apply) Plane Train Car Bus Bike Hike RV MC

I went with:

We stayed in (space, cabin # etc):

Most relaxing day:

Something funny:

Someone we met:

Best story told:

The kids liked this:

The best food:

Games played:

Something disappointing:

Next time I'll do this differently:

Medoc Mountain State Park
City: Hollister   County: Halifax

Plan your trip: https://www.ncparks.gov/medoc-mountain-state-park/home

Activities:

- ❑ Biking
- ❑ Boating
- ❑ Disc Golf
- ❑ Fishing
- ❑ Gold Panning
- ❑ Hiking
- ❑ Historic Learning
- ❑ Horseback Riding
- ❑ Hunting
- ❑ Kite Boarding
- ❑ Metal Detecting
- ❑ OHV
- ❑ Paddling
- ❑ Rock Climbing
- ❑ Stargazing
- ❑ Swimming
- ❑ Wildlife Viewing
- ❑ Windsurfing
- ❑
- ❑
- ❑
- ❑
- ❑
- ❑
- ❑
- ❑
- ❑
- ❑
- ❑
- ❑

Facilities:

- ❑ ADA
- ❑ Picnic sites
- ❑ Restrooms
- ❑ Showers
- ❑ Trailer Access
- ❑ Visitor center
- ❑ Group Camping
- ❑ RV Camp
- ❑ Rustic Camping
- ❑ Cabins / Yurts
- ❑ Day Use Area

Notes:

Get the Facts

- ❑ Phone   252-586-6588
- ❑ Park Hours

  _____

- ❑ Reservations? ____Y ____N

  date made_____

- ❑ Open all year ____Y_____N

  dates_____

- ❑ Check in time _____
- ❑ Check out time _____
- ❑ Pet friendly _____Y _____N
- ❑ Max RV length _____
- ❑ Distance from home

  miles: _____

  hours: _____

- ❑ Address_____

  _____

  _____

Fees:

- ❑ Day Use $ _____
- ❑ Camp Sites $ _____
- ❑ RV Sites $ _____
- ❑ Refund policy

  _____

  _____

  _____

Make It Personal

Trip dates: The weather was: Sunny   Cloudy   Rainy   Stormy   Snowy   Foggy   Warm   Cold

Why I went:

How I got there: (circle all that apply)   Plane   Train   Car   Bus   Bike   Hike   RV   MC

I went with:

We stayed in (space, cabin # etc):

Most relaxing day:

Something funny:

Someone we met:

Best story told:

The kids liked this:

The best food:

Games played:

Something disappointing:

Next time I'll do this differently:

Raven Rock State Park
City: Lillington   County: Harnett
Plan your trip: https://www.ncparks.gov/raven-rock-state-park/home

Activities:

- ❑ Biking
- ❑ Boating
- ❑ Disc Golf
- ❑ Fishing
- ❑ Gold Panning
- ❑ Hiking
- ❑ Historic Learning
- ❑ Horseback Riding
- ❑ Hunting
- ❑ Kite Boarding
- ❑ Metal Detecting
- ❑ OHV
- ❑ Paddling
- ❑ Rock Climbing
- ❑ Stargazing
- ❑ Swimming
- ❑ Wildlife Viewing
- ❑ Windsurfing
- ❑
- ❑
- ❑
- ❑
- ❑
- ❑
- ❑
- ❑
- ❑
- ❑
- ❑
- ❑

Facilities:

- ❑ ADA
- ❑ Picnic sites
- ❑ Restrooms
- ❑ Showers
- ❑ Trailer Access
- ❑ Visitor center
- ❑ Group Camping
- ❑ RV Camp
- ❑ Rustic Camping
- ❑ Cabins / Yurts
- ❑ Day Use Area

Notes:

Get the Facts

- ❑ Phone   910-893-4888
- ❑ Park Hours

  _____

- ❑ Reservations? ____Y ____N

  date made_____

- ❑ Open all year ____Y____N

  dates_____

- ❑ Check in time _____
- ❑ Check out time _____
- ❑ Pet friendly _____Y _____N
- ❑ Max RV length _____
- ❑ Distance from home

  miles: _____

  hours: _____

- ❑ Address_____

  _____

  _____

Fees:

- ❑ Day Use $ _____
- ❑ Camp Sites $ _____
- ❑ RV Sites $ _____
- ❑ Refund policy

  _____

  _____

  _____

Make It Personal

Trip dates:

The weather was: Sunny Cloudy Rainy Stormy Snowy Foggy Warm Cold

Why I went:

How I got there: (circle all that apply) Plane Train Car Bus Bike Hike RV MC

I went with:

We stayed in (space, cabin # etc):

Most relaxing day:

Something funny:

Someone we met:

Best story told:

The kids liked this:

The best food:

Games played:

Something disappointing:

Next time I'll do this differently:

Lake Norman State Park
City: Troutman   County: Iredell
Plan your trip: https://www.ncparks.gov/lake-norman-state-park/home

Activities:

- ❑ Biking
- ❑ Boating
- ❑ Disc Golf
- ❑ Fishing
- ❑ Gold Panning
- ❑ Hiking
- ❑ Historic Learning
- ❑ Horseback Riding
- ❑ Hunting
- ❑ Kite Boarding

- ❑ Metal Detecting
- ❑ OHV
- ❑ Paddling
- ❑ Rock Climbing
- ❑ Stargazing
- ❑ Swimming
- ❑ Wildlife Viewing
- ❑ Windsurfing
- ❑
- ❑

- ❑
- ❑
- ❑
- ❑
- ❑
- ❑
- ❑
- ❑
- ❑
- ❑

Facilities:

- ❑ ADA
- ❑ Picnic sites
- ❑ Restrooms
- ❑ Showers
- ❑ Trailer Access
- ❑ Visitor center
- ❑ Group Camping
- ❑ RV Camp
- ❑ Rustic Camping
- ❑ Cabins / Yurts
- ❑ Day Use Area

Notes:

Get the Facts

- ❑ Phone   704-528-6350
- ❑ Park Hours

  _____

- ❑ Reservations? ____Y ____N

  date made_____
- ❑ Open all year ____Y____N

  dates_____
- ❑ Check in time _____
- ❑ Check out time _____
- ❑ Pet friendly _____Y _____N
- ❑ Max RV length _____
- ❑ Distance from home

  miles: _____

  hours: _____
- ❑ Address_____

  _____

  _____

Fees:

- ❑ Day Use $ _____
- ❑ Camp Sites $ _____
- ❑ RV Sites $ _____
- ❑ Refund policy

  _____

  _____

  _____

Make It Personal

Trip dates:

The weather was: Sunny Cloudy Rainy Stormy Snowy Foggy Warm Cold

Why I went:

How I got there: (circle all that apply)   Plane   Train   Car   Bus   Bike   Hike   RV   MC

I went with:

We stayed in (space, cabin # etc):

Most relaxing day:

Something funny:

Someone we met:

Best story told:

The kids liked this:

The best food:

Games played:

Something disappointing:

Next time I'll do this differently:

Lumber River State Park

City: Orrum   County: Robeson

Plan your trip: https://www.ncparks.gov/lumber-river-state-park/home

Activities:

- ❏ Biking
- ❏ Boating
- ❏ Disc Golf
- ❏ Fishing
- ❏ Gold Panning
- ❏ Hiking
- ❏ Historic Learning
- ❏ Horseback Riding
- ❏ Hunting
- ❏ Kite Boarding

- ❏ Metal Detecting
- ❏ OHV
- ❏ Paddling
- ❏ Rock Climbing
- ❏ Stargazing
- ❏ Swimming
- ❏ Wildlife Viewing
- ❏ Windsurfing
- ❏
- ❏

- ❏
- ❏
- ❏
- ❏
- ❏
- ❏
- ❏
- ❏
- ❏
- ❏

Facilities:

- ❏ ADA
- ❏ Picnic sites
- ❏ Restrooms
- ❏ Showers
- ❏ Trailer Access
- ❏ Visitor center
- ❏ Group Camping
- ❏ RV Camp
- ❏ Rustic Camping
- ❏ Cabins / Yurts
- ❏ Day Use Area

Notes:

Get the Facts

- ❏ Phone   910-628-4564
- ❏ Park Hours

  _____

- ❏ Reservations? ____Y ____N

  date made_____
- ❏ Open all year ____Y____N

  dates_____
- ❏ Check in time _____
- ❏ Check out time _____
- ❏ Pet friendly _____Y _____N
- ❏ Max RV length _____
- ❏ Distance from home

  miles: _____

  hours: _____
- ❏ Address_____

  _____

  _____

Fees:

- ❏ Day Use $ _____
- ❏ Camp Sites $ _____
- ❏ RV Sites $ _____
- ❏ Refund policy

  _____

  _____

  _____

Make It Personal

Trip dates:

The weather was: Sunny Cloudy Rainy Stormy Snowy Foggy Warm Cold

Why I went:

How I got there: (circle all that apply) Plane Train Car Bus Bike Hike RV MC

I went with:

We stayed in (space, cabin # etc):

Most relaxing day:

Something funny:

Someone we met:

Best story told:

The kids liked this:

The best food:

Games played:

Something disappointing:

Next time I'll do this differently:

Mayo River State Park
City: Mayodan   County: Rockingham
Plan your trip: https://www.ncparks.gov/mayo-river-state-park/home

Activities:

- ☐ Biking
- ☐ Boating
- ☐ Disc Golf
- ☐ Fishing
- ☐ Gold Panning
- ☐ Hiking
- ☐ Historic Learning
- ☐ Horseback Riding
- ☐ Hunting
- ☐ Kite Boarding

- ☐ Metal Detecting
- ☐ OHV
- ☐ Paddling
- ☐ Rock Climbing
- ☐ Stargazing
- ☐ Swimming
- ☐ Wildlife Viewing
- ☐ Windsurfing
- ☐
- ☐

- ☐
- ☐
- ☐
- ☐
- ☐
- ☐
- ☐
- ☐
- ☐
- ☐

Facilities:

- ☐ ADA
- ☐ Picnic sites
- ☐ Restrooms
- ☐ Showers
- ☐ Trailer Access
- ☐ Visitor center
- ☐ Group Camping
- ☐ RV Camp
- ☐ Rustic Camping
- ☐ Cabins / Yurts
- ☐ Day Use Area

Notes:

Get the Facts

- ☐ Phone   336-427-2530
- ☐ Park Hours

  _____

- ☐ Reservations? ____Y ____N

  date made_____

- ☐ Open all year ____Y ____N

  dates_____

- ☐ Check in time _____
- ☐ Check out time _____
- ☐ Pet friendly _____Y _____N
- ☐ Max RV length _____
- ☐ Distance from home

  miles: _____

  hours: _____

- ☐ Address_____

  _____

  _____

Fees:

- ☐ Day Use $ _____
- ☐ Camp Sites $ _____
- ☐ RV Sites $ _____
- ☐ Refund policy

  _____

  _____

  _____

Make It Personal

Trip dates:

The weather was: Sunny Cloudy Rainy Stormy Snowy Foggy Warm Cold

Why I went:

How I got there: (circle all that apply) Plane Train Car Bus Bike Hike RV MC

I went with:

We stayed in (space, cabin # etc):

Most relaxing day:

Something funny:

Someone we met:

Best story told:

The kids liked this:

The best food:

Games played:

Something disappointing:

Next time I'll do this differently:

Morrow Mountain State Park
City: Albemarle   County: Stanly
Plan your trip: https://www.ncparks.gov/morrow-mountain-state-park/home

Activities:

- ❑ Biking
- ❑ Boating
- ❑ Disc Golf
- ❑ Fishing
- ❑ Gold Panning
- ❑ Hiking
- ❑ Historic Learning
- ❑ Horseback Riding
- ❑ Hunting
- ❑ Kite Boarding

- ❑ Metal Detecting
- ❑ OHV
- ❑ Paddling
- ❑ Rock Climbing
- ❑ Stargazing
- ❑ Swimming
- ❑ Wildlife Viewing
- ❑ Windsurfing
- ❑
- ❑

- ❑
- ❑
- ❑
- ❑
- ❑
- ❑
- ❑
- ❑
- ❑
- ❑

Facilities:

- ❑ ADA
- ❑ Picnic sites
- ❑ Restrooms
- ❑ Showers
- ❑ Trailer Access
- ❑ Visitor center
- ❑ Group Camping
- ❑ RV Camp
- ❑ Rustic Camping
- ❑ Cabins / Yurts
- ❑ Day Use Area

Notes:

Get the Facts

- ❑ Phone   704-982-4402
- ❑ Park Hours

  _____

- ❑ Reservations? ____Y ____N

  date made_____

- ❑ Open all year ____Y_____N

  dates_____

- ❑ Check in time _____

- ❑ Check out time _____

- ❑ Pet friendly _____Y _____N

- ❑ Max RV length _____

- ❑ Distance from home

  miles: _____

  hours: _____

- ❑ Address_____

  _____

  _____

Fees:

- ❑ Day Use $ _____
- ❑ Camp Sites $ _____
- ❑ RV Sites $ _____
- ❑ Refund policy

  _____

  _____

  _____

Make It Personal

Trip dates: _____

The weather was: Sunny Cloudy Rainy Stormy Snowy Foggy Warm Cold

Why I went:
_____

How I got there: (circle all that apply) Plane Train Car Bus Bike Hike RV MC

I went with:
_____

We stayed in (space, cabin # etc):
_____

Most relaxing day:
_____

Something funny:
_____

Someone we met:
_____

Best story told:
_____

The kids liked this:
_____

The best food:
_____

Games played:
_____

Something disappointing:
_____

Next time I'll do this differently:
_____
_____

Pilot Mountain State Park
City: Pinnacle   County: Stokes

Plan your trip: https://www.ncparks.gov/pilot-mountain-state-park/home

Activities:

- ❑ Biking
- ❑ Boating
- ❑ Disc Golf
- ❑ Fishing
- ❑ Gold Panning
- ❑ Hiking
- ❑ Historic Learning
- ❑ Horseback Riding
- ❑ Hunting
- ❑ Kite Boarding

- ❑ Metal Detecting
- ❑ OHV
- ❑ Paddling
- ❑ Rock Climbing
- ❑ Stargazing
- ❑ Swimming
- ❑ Wildlife Viewing
- ❑ Windsurfing
- ❑
- ❑

- ❑
- ❑
- ❑
- ❑
- ❑
- ❑
- ❑
- ❑
- ❑
- ❑

Facilities:

- ❑ ADA
- ❑ Picnic sites
- ❑ Restrooms
- ❑ Showers
- ❑ Trailer Access
- ❑ Visitor center
- ❑ Group Camping
- ❑ RV Camp
- ❑ Rustic Camping
- ❑ Cabins / Yurts
- ❑ Day Use Area

Notes:

Get the Facts

- ❑ Phone   336-444-5100
- ❑ Park Hours

  _____

- ❑ Reservations? _____Y _____N

  date made_____

- ❑ Open all year _____Y_____N

  dates_____

- ❑ Check in time _____
- ❑ Check out time _____
- ❑ Pet friendly _____Y _____N
- ❑ Max RV length _____
- ❑ Distance from home

  miles: _____

  hours: _____

- ❑ Address_____

  _____

  _____

Fees:

- ❑ Day Use $ _____
- ❑ Camp Sites $ _____
- ❑ RV Sites $ _____
- ❑ Refund policy

  _____

  _____

  _____

Make It Personal

Trip dates:

The weather was: Sunny Cloudy Rainy Stormy Snowy Foggy Warm Cold

Why I went:

How I got there: (circle all that apply) Plane Train Car Bus Bike Hike RV MC

I went with:

We stayed in (space, cabin # etc):

Most relaxing day:

Something funny:

Someone we met:

Best story told:

The kids liked this:

The best food:

Games played:

Something disappointing:

Next time I'll do this differently:

Kerr Lake State Recreation Area
City: Henderson   County: Vance

Plan your trip: https://www.ncparks.gov/kerr-lake-state-recreation-area/home

Activities:

- ❑ Biking
- ❑ Boating
- ❑ Disc Golf
- ❑ Fishing
- ❑ Gold Panning
- ❑ Hiking
- ❑ Historic Learning
- ❑ Horseback Riding
- ❑ Hunting
- ❑ Kite Boarding

- ❑ Metal Detecting
- ❑ OHV
- ❑ Paddling
- ❑ Rock Climbing
- ❑ Stargazing
- ❑ Swimming
- ❑ Wildlife Viewing
- ❑ Windsurfing
- ❑
- ❑

- ❑
- ❑
- ❑
- ❑
- ❑
- ❑
- ❑
- ❑
- ❑
- ❑

Facilities:

- ❑ ADA
- ❑ Picnic sites
- ❑ Restrooms
- ❑ Showers
- ❑ Trailer Access
- ❑ Visitor center
- ❑ Group Camping
- ❑ RV Camp
- ❑ Rustic Camping
- ❑ Cabins / Yurts
- ❑ Day Use Area

Notes:

Get the Facts

- ❑ Phone   252-438-7791
- ❑ Park Hours

  _____

- ❑ Reservations? ____Y ____N

  date made_____

- ❑ Open all year ____Y____N

  dates_____

- ❑ Check in time _____
- ❑ Check out time _____
- ❑ Pet friendly _____Y _____N
- ❑ Max RV length _____
- ❑ Distance from home

  miles: _____

  hours: _____

- ❑ Address_____

  _____

  _____

Fees:

- ❑ Day Use $ _____
- ❑ Camp Sites $ _____
- ❑ RV Sites $ _____
- ❑ Refund policy

  _____

  _____

  _____

Make It Personal

Trip dates: _____

The weather was: Sunny Cloudy Rainy Stormy Snowy Foggy Warm Cold

Why I went: _____
_____

How I got there: (circle all that apply) Plane Train Car Bus Bike Hike RV MC

I went with: _____

We stayed in (space, cabin # etc): _____

Most relaxing day: _____
_____

Something funny: _____
_____

Someone we met: _____
_____

Best story told: _____
_____

The kids liked this: _____
_____

The best food: _____
_____

Games played: _____
_____

Something disappointing: _____
_____

Next time I'll do this differently: _____
_____

Jordan Lake State Recreation Area
City: Apex   County: Wake

Plan your trip: https://www.ncparks.gov/jordan-lake-state-recreation-area/home

Activities:

- ❑ Biking
- ❑ Boating
- ❑ Disc Golf
- ❑ Fishing
- ❑ Gold Panning
- ❑ Hiking
- ❑ Historic Learning
- ❑ Horseback Riding
- ❑ Hunting
- ❑ Kite Boarding

- ❑ Metal Detecting
- ❑ OHV
- ❑ Paddling
- ❑ Rock Climbing
- ❑ Stargazing
- ❑ Swimming
- ❑ Wildlife Viewing
- ❑ Windsurfing
- ❑
- ❑

- ❑
- ❑
- ❑
- ❑
- ❑
- ❑
- ❑
- ❑
- ❑
- ❑

Facilities:

- ❑ ADA
- ❑ Picnic sites
- ❑ Restrooms
- ❑ Showers
- ❑ Trailer Access
- ❑ Visitor center
- ❑ Group Camping
- ❑ RV Camp
- ❑ Rustic Camping
- ❑ Cabins / Yurts
- ❑ Day Use Area

Notes:

Get the Facts

- ❑ Phone   919-362-0586
- ❑ Park Hours

  _____

- ❑ Reservations? ____Y ____N

  date made_____

- ❑ Open all year ____Y____N

  dates_____

- ❑ Check in time _____

- ❑ Check out time _____

- ❑ Pet friendly _____Y _____N

- ❑ Max RV length _____

- ❑ Distance from home

  miles: _____

  hours: _____

- ❑ Address_____

  _____

  _____

Fees:

- ❑ Day Use $ _____
- ❑ Camp Sites $ _____
- ❑ RV Sites $ _____
- ❑ Refund policy

  _____

  _____

  _____

Make It Personal

Trip dates:

The weather was: Sunny Cloudy Rainy Stormy Snowy Foggy Warm Cold

Why I went:

How I got there: (circle all that apply) Plane Train Car Bus Bike Hike RV MC

I went with:

We stayed in (space, cabin # etc):

Most relaxing day:

Something funny:

Someone we met:

Best story told:

The kids liked this:

The best food:

Games played:

Something disappointing:

Next time I'll do this differently:

William B. Umstead State Park

City: Raleigh   **County: Wake**

Plan your trip: https://www.ncparks.gov/william-b-umstead-state-park/home

Activities:

- ❏ Biking
- ❏ Boating
- ❏ Disc Golf
- ❏ Fishing
- ❏ Gold Panning
- ❏ Hiking
- ❏ Historic Learning
- ❏ Horseback Riding
- ❏ Hunting
- ❏ Kite Boarding

- ❏ Metal Detecting
- ❏ OHV
- ❏ Paddling
- ❏ Rock Climbing
- ❏ Stargazing
- ❏ Swimming
- ❏ Wildlife Viewing
- ❏ Windsurfing
- ❏
- ❏

- ❏
- ❏
- ❏
- ❏
- ❏
- ❏
- ❏
- ❏
- ❏
- ❏

Facilities:

- ❏ ADA
- ❏ Picnic sites
- ❏ Restrooms
- ❏ Showers
- ❏ Trailer Access
- ❏ Visitor center
- ❏ Group Camping
- ❏ RV Camp
- ❏ Rustic Camping
- ❏ Cabins / Yurts
- ❏ Day Use Area

Notes:

Get the Facts

- ❏ Phone   919-571-4170
- ❏ Park Hours

  _____

- ❏ Reservations? ____Y ____N

  date made_____

- ❏ Open all year ____Y____N

  dates_____

- ❏ Check in time _____

- ❏ Check out time _____

- ❏ Pet friendly _____Y _____N

- ❏ Max RV length _____

- ❏ Distance from home

  miles: _____

  hours: _____

- ❏ Address_____

  _____

  _____

Fees:

- ❏ Day Use $ _____
- ❏ Camp Sites $ _____
- ❏ RV Sites $ _____
- ❏ Refund policy

  _____

  _____

  _____

Make It Personal

Trip dates: _____ | The weather was: Sunny Cloudy Rainy Stormy Snowy Foggy Warm Cold

Why I went:
_____

How I got there: (circle all that apply)   Plane   Train   Car   Bus   Bike   Hike   RV   MC

I went with:
_____

We stayed in (space, cabin # etc):
_____

Most relaxing day:
_____

Something funny:
_____

Someone we met:
_____

Best story told:
_____

The kids liked this:
_____

The best food:
_____

Games played:
_____

Something disappointing:
_____

Next time I'll do this differently:
_____
_____

Falls Lake State Recreation Area
City: Wake Forest   County: Wake

Plan your trip: https://www.ncparks.gov/falls-lake-state-recreation-area/home

Activities:

- ❑ Biking
- ❑ Boating
- ❑ Disc Golf
- ❑ Fishing
- ❑ Gold Panning
- ❑ Hiking
- ❑ Historic Learning
- ❑ Horseback Riding
- ❑ Hunting
- ❑ Kite Boarding

- ❑ Metal Detecting
- ❑ OHV
- ❑ Paddling
- ❑ Rock Climbing
- ❑ Stargazing
- ❑ Swimming
- ❑ Wildlife Viewing
- ❑ Windsurfing
- ❑
- ❑

- ❑
- ❑
- ❑
- ❑
- ❑
- ❑
- ❑
- ❑
- ❑
- ❑

Facilities:

- ❑ ADA
- ❑ Picnic sites
- ❑ Restrooms
- ❑ Showers
- ❑ Trailer Access
- ❑ Visitor center
- ❑ Group Camping
- ❑ RV Camp
- ❑ Rustic Camping
- ❑ Cabins / Yurts
- ❑ Day Use Area

Notes:

Get the Facts

- ❑ Phone   910-458-5798
- ❑ Park Hours

  _____

- ❑ Reservations? ____Y ____N

  date made_____

- ❑ Open all year ____Y_____N

  dates_____

- ❑ Check in time _____

- ❑ Check out time _____

- ❑ Pet friendly _____Y _____N

- ❑ Max RV length _____

- ❑ Distance from home

  miles: _____

  hours: _____

- ❑ Address_____

  _____

  _____

Fees:

- ❑ Day Use $ _____
- ❑ Camp Sites $ _____
- ❑ RV Sites $ _____
- ❑ Refund policy

  _____

  _____

  _____

Make It Personal

Trip dates:

The weather was: Sunny Cloudy Rainy Stormy Snowy Foggy Warm Cold

Why I went:

How I got there: (circle all that apply)   Plane   Train   Car   Bus   Bike   Hike   RV   MC

I went with:

We stayed in (space, cabin # etc):

Most relaxing day:

Something funny:

Someone we met:

Best story told:

The kids liked this:

The best food:

Games played:

Something disappointing:

Next time I'll do this differently:

Cliffs of the Neuse State Park
City: Seven Springs   County: Wayne
Plan your trip: https://www.ncparks.gov/cliffs-of-the-neuse-state-park/home

Activities:

- ❏ Biking
- ❏ Boating
- ❏ Disc Golf
- ❏ Fishing
- ❏ Gold Panning
- ❏ Hiking
- ❏ Historic Learning
- ❏ Horseback Riding
- ❏ Hunting
- ❏ Kite Boarding

- ❏ Metal Detecting
- ❏ OHV
- ❏ Paddling
- ❏ Rock Climbing
- ❏ Stargazing
- ❏ Swimming
- ❏ Wildlife Viewing
- ❏ Windsurfing
- ❏
- ❏

- ❏
- ❏
- ❏
- ❏
- ❏
- ❏
- ❏
- ❏
- ❏
- ❏

Facilities:

- ❏ ADA
- ❏ Picnic sites
- ❏ Restrooms
- ❏ Showers
- ❏ Trailer Access
- ❏ Visitor center
- ❏ Group Camping
- ❏ RV Camp
- ❏ Rustic Camping
- ❏ Cabins / Yurts
- ❏ Day Use Area

Notes:

Get the Facts

- ❏ Phone   919-778-6234
- ❏ Park Hours

  _____

- ❏ Reservations? _____Y _____N

  date made_____

- ❏ Open all year _____Y_____N

  dates_____

- ❏ Check in time _____

- ❏ Check out time _____

- ❏ Pet friendly _____Y _____N

- ❏ Max RV length _____

- ❏ Distance from home

  miles: _____

  hours: _____

- ❏ Address_____

  _____

  _____

Fees:

- ❏ Day Use $ _____
- ❏ Camp Sites $ _____
- ❏ RV Sites $ _____
- ❏ Refund policy

  _____

  _____

  _____

Make It Personal

Trip dates:

The weather was: Sunny Cloudy Rainy Stormy Snowy Foggy Warm Cold

Why I went:

How I got there: (circle all that apply)   Plane   Train   Car   Bus   Bike   Hike   RV   MC

I went with:

We stayed in (space, cabin # etc):

Most relaxing day:

Something funny:

Someone we met:

Best story told:

The kids liked this:

The best food:

Games played:

Something disappointing:

Next time I'll do this differently:

Reed Gold Mine Historic Site
City: Midland   County: Cabarrus
Plan your trip: https://historicsites.nc.gov/node/64

Activities:

- ❑ ATV / OHV   ❑
- ❑ Bike Trails   ❑
- ❑ Birding   ❑
- ❑ Boating   ❑
- ❑ Fishing   ❑
- ❑ Hiking   ❑
- ❑ Horseback   ❑
- ❑ Mountain Biking   ❑
- ❑ Watersports   ❑
- ❑ Wildlife   ❑
- ❑ Winter Sports

Facilities:

- ❑ ADA   ❑
- ❑ Gift Shop   ❑
- ❑ Museum   ❑
- ❑ Visitor Center   ❑
- ❑ Picnic sites   ❑
- ❑ Restrooms   ❑

Things to do in the area:

Get the Facts

- ❑ Phone   704-721-4653
- ❑ Park Hours

  _____

- ❑ Reservations? _____Y _____N

  date made_____

- ❑ Open all year? _____Y_____N

  dates_____

- ❑ Dog friendly _____Y _____N

- ❑ Distance from home

  miles: _____

  hours: _____

- ❑ Address_____

  _____

  _____

Fees:

- ❑ Day Use $ _____
- ❑ Refund policy

  _____

  _____

  _____

Notes:

Carvers Creek State Park

City: Spring Lake   **County: Cumberland**

Plan your trip: https://www.ncparks.gov/carvers-creek-state-park/home

Activities:

- ❑ ATV / OHV ❑
- ❑ Bike Trails ❑
- ❑ Birding ❑
- ❑ Boating ❑
- ❑ Fishing ❑
- ❑ Hiking ❑
- ❑ Horseback ❑
- ❑ Mountain Biking ❑
- ❑ Watersports ❑
- ❑ Wildlife ❑
- ❑ Winter Sports

Facilities:

- ❑ ADA ❑
- ❑ Gift Shop ❑
- ❑ Museum ❑
- ❑ Visitor Center ❑
- ❑ Picnic sites ❑
- ❑ Restrooms ❑

Things to do in the area:

Get the Facts

- ❑ Phone 910-436-4681
- ❑ Park Hours

  _____

- ❑ Reservations? ____Y ____N

  date made_____

- ❑ Open all year? ____Y____N

  dates_____

- ❑ Dog friendly _____Y _____N

- ❑ Distance from home

  miles: _____

  hours: _____

- ❑ Address_____

  _____

  _____

Fees:

- ❑ Day Use $ _____
- ❑ Refund policy

  _____

  _____

  _____

Notes:

Bennett Place Historic Site
City: Durham   County: Durham

Plan your trip: https://historicsites.nc.gov/node/71

Activities:

- ❑ ATV / OHV   ❑
- ❑ Bike Trails   ❑
- ❑ Birding   ❑
- ❑ Boating   ❑
- ❑ Fishing   ❑
- ❑ Hiking   ❑
- ❑ Horseback   ❑
- ❑ Mountain Biking   ❑
- ❑ Watersports   ❑
- ❑ Wildlife   ❑
- ❑ Winter Sports

Facilities:

- ❑ ADA   ❑
- ❑ Gift Shop   ❑
- ❑ Museum   ❑
- ❑ Visitor Center   ❑
- ❑ Picnic sites   ❑
- ❑ Restrooms   ❑

Things to do in the area:

Get the Facts

- ❑ Phone   919-383-4345
- ❑ Park Hours

  _____

- ❑ Reservations? ____Y ____N

  date made_____

- ❑ Open all year? ____Y____N

  dates_____

- ❑ Dog friendly _____Y _____N

- ❑ Distance from home

  miles: _____

  hours: _____

- ❑ Address_____

  _____

  _____

Fees:

- ❑ Day Use $ _____
- ❑ Refund policy

  _____

  _____

  _____

Notes:

Duke Homestead Historic Site
City: Durham   County: Durham
Plan your trip: https://historicsites.nc.gov/node/53

Activities:

- [ ] ATV / OHV   [ ]
- [ ] Bike Trails   [ ]
- [ ] Birding   [ ]
- [ ] Boating   [ ]
- [ ] Fishing   [ ]
- [ ] Hiking   [ ]
- [ ] Horseback   [ ]
- [ ] Mountain Biking   [ ]
- [ ] Watersports   [ ]
- [ ] Wildlife   [ ]
- [ ] Winter Sports

Facilities:

- [ ] ADA   [ ]
- [ ] Gift Shop   [ ]
- [ ] Museum   [ ]
- [ ] Visitor Center   [ ]
- [ ] Picnic sites   [ ]
- [ ] Restrooms   [ ]

Things to do in the area:

Get the Facts

- [ ] Phone   919-477-5498
- [ ] Park Hours

  _____

- [ ] Reservations? _____Y _____N

  date made_____

- [ ] Open all year? _____Y_____N

  dates_____

- [ ] Dog friendly _____Y _____N
- [ ] Distance from home

  miles: _____

  hours: _____

- [ ] Address_____

  _____

  _____

Fees:

- [ ] Day Use $ _____
- [ ] Refund policy

  _____

  _____

  _____

Notes:

Historic Stagville Historic Site
City: Durham   County: Durham

Plan your trip: https://historicsites.nc.gov/node/59

Activities:

- ❑ ATV / OHV   ❑
- ❑ Bike Trails   ❑
- ❑ Birding   ❑
- ❑ Boating   ❑
- ❑ Fishing   ❑
- ❑ Hiking   ❑
- ❑ Horseback   ❑
- ❑ Mountain Biking   ❑
- ❑ Watersports   ❑
- ❑ Wildlife   ❑
- ❑ Winter Sports

Facilities:

- ❑ ADA   ❑
- ❑ Gift Shop   ❑
- ❑ Museum   ❑
- ❑ Visitor Center   ❑
- ❑ Picnic sites   ❑
- ❑ Restrooms   ❑

Things to do in the area:

Get the Facts

- ❑ Phone   919-620-0120
- ❑ Park Hours

  _____

- ❑ Reservations? ____Y ____N

  date made_____

- ❑ Open all year? ____Y____N

  dates_____

- ❑ Dog friendly _____Y _____N

- ❑ Distance from home

  miles: _____

  hours: _____

- ❑ Address_____

  _____

  _____

Fees:

- ❑ Day Use $ _____
- ❑ Refund policy

  _____

  _____

  _____

Notes:

Alamance Battleground Historic Site
City: Burlington   County: Guilford

Plan your trip: https://historicsites.nc.gov/all-sites/alamance-battleground

Activities:

- ❑ ATV / OHV ❑
- ❑ Bike Trails ❑
- ❑ Birding ❑
- ❑ Boating ❑
- ❑ Fishing ❑
- ❑ Hiking ❑
- ❑ Horseback ❑
- ❑ Mountain Biking ❑
- ❑ Watersports ❑
- ❑ Wildlife ❑
- ❑ Winter Sports

Facilities:

- ❑ ADA ❑
- ❑ Gift Shop ❑
- ❑ Museum ❑
- ❑ Visitor Center ❑
- ❑ Picnic sites ❑
- ❑ Restrooms ❑

Things to do in the area:

Get the Facts

- ❑ Phone   336-227-4785
- ❑ Park Hours

    _____

- ❑ Reservations? ____Y ____N

    date made_____

- ❑ Open all year? ____Y____N

    dates_____

- ❑ Dog friendly _____Y _____N

- ❑ Distance from home

    miles: _____

    hours: _____

- ❑ Address_____

    _____

    _____

Fees:

- ❑ Day Use $ _____
- ❑ Refund policy

    _____

    _____

    _____

Notes:

Charlotte Hawkins Brown Museum Historic Site
City: Gibsonville   County: Guilford
Plan your trip: https://historicsites.nc.gov/node/51

Activities:

- ❑ ATV / OHV   ❑
- ❑ Bike Trails   ❑
- ❑ Birding   ❑
- ❑ Boating   ❑
- ❑ Fishing   ❑
- ❑ Hiking   ❑
- ❑ Horseback   ❑
- ❑ Mountain Biking   ❑
- ❑ Watersports   ❑
- ❑ Wildlife   ❑
- ❑ Winter Sports

Facilities:

- ❑ ADA   ❑
- ❑ Gift Shop   ❑
- ❑ Museum   ❑
- ❑ Visitor Center   ❑
- ❑ Picnic sites   ❑
- ❑ Restrooms   ❑

Things to do in the area:

Get the Facts

- ❑ Phone   336-449-3310
- ❑ Park Hours

  _____

- ❑ Reservations? ____Y ____N

  date made_____

- ❑ Open all year? ____Y____N

  dates_____

- ❑ Dog friendly _____Y _____N

- ❑ Distance from home

  miles: _____

  hours: _____

- ❑ Address_____

  _____

  _____

Fees:

- ❑ Day Use $ _____
- ❑ Refund policy

  _____

  _____

  _____

Notes:

Historic Halifax

City: Halifax

County: Halifax

Plan your trip: https://historicsites.nc.gov/node/58

Activities:

- ❑ ATV / OHV ❑
- ❑ Bike Trails ❑
- ❑ Birding ❑
- ❑ Boating ❑
- ❑ Fishing ❑
- ❑ Hiking ❑
- ❑ Horseback ❑
- ❑ Mountain Biking ❑
- ❑ Watersports ❑
- ❑ Wildlife ❑
- ❑ Winter Sports

Facilities:

- ❑ ADA ❑
- ❑ Gift Shop ❑
- ❑ Museum ❑
- ❑ Visitor Center ❑
- ❑ Picnic sites ❑
- ❑ Restrooms ❑

Things to do in the area:

Get the Facts

- ❑ Phone   252-583-7191
- ❑ Park Hours

  _____

- ❑ Reservations? ____Y ____N

  date made_____

- ❑ Open all year? ____Y____N

  dates_____

- ❑ Dog friendly _____Y _____N

- ❑ Distance from home

  miles: _____

  hours: _____

- ❑ Address_____

  _____

  _____

Fees:

- ❑ Day Use $ _____
- ❑ Refund policy

  _____

  _____

  _____

Notes:

Fort Dobbs Historic Site
City: Statesville   County: Iredell
Plan your trip: https://historicsites.nc.gov/node/54

Activities:

- [ ] ATV / OHV   [ ]
- [ ] Bike Trails   [ ]
- [ ] Birding   [ ]
- [ ] Boating   [ ]
- [ ] Fishing   [ ]
- [ ] Hiking   [ ]
- [ ] Horseback   [ ]
- [ ] Mountain Biking   [ ]
- [ ] Watersports   [ ]
- [ ] Wildlife   [ ]
- [ ] Winter Sports

Facilities:

- [ ] ADA   [ ]
- [ ] Gift Shop   [ ]
- [ ] Museum   [ ]
- [ ] Visitor Center   [ ]
- [ ] Picnic sites   [ ]
- [ ] Restrooms   [ ]

Things to do in the area:

Get the Facts

- [ ] Phone   704-873-5882
- [ ] Park Hours

  _____

- [ ] Reservations? _____Y _____N

  date made_____

- [ ] Open all year? _____Y_____N

  dates_____

- [ ] Dog friendly _____Y _____N

- [ ] Distance from home

  miles: _____

  hours: _____

- [ ] Address_____

  _____

  _____

Fees:

- [ ] Day Use $ _____
- [ ] Refund policy

  _____

  _____

  _____

Notes:

Bentonville Battlefield Historic Site

City: Four Oaks   County: Johnston

Plan your trip: https://historicsites.nc.gov/node/49

Activities:

- ❑ ATV / OHV   ❑
- ❑ Bike Trails   ❑
- ❑ Birding   ❑
- ❑ Boating   ❑
- ❑ Fishing   ❑
- ❑ Hiking   ❑
- ❑ Horseback   ❑
- ❑ Mountain Biking   ❑
- ❑ Watersports   ❑
- ❑ Wildlife   ❑
- ❑ Winter Sports

Facilities:

- ❑ ADA   ❑
- ❑ Gift Shop   ❑
- ❑ Museum   ❑
- ❑ Visitor Center   ❑
- ❑ Picnic sites   ❑
- ❑ Restrooms   ❑

Things to do in the area:

Get the Facts

- ❑ Phone   910-594-0789
- ❑ Park Hours

  _____

- ❑ Reservations? _____Y _____N

  date made_____

- ❑ Open all year? _____Y_____N

  dates_____

- ❑ Dog friendly _____Y _____N

- ❑ Distance from home

  miles: _____

  hours: _____

- ❑ Address_____

  _____

  _____

Fees:

- ❑ Day Use $ _____
- ❑ Refund policy

  _____

  _____

  _____

Notes:

House in the Horseshoe Historic Site
City: Sanford   County: Lee

Plan your trip: https://historicsites.nc.gov/node/61

Activities:

- ❑ ATV / OHV   ❑
- ❑ Bike Trails   ❑
- ❑ Birding   ❑
- ❑ Boating   ❑
- ❑ Fishing   ❑
- ❑ Hiking   ❑
- ❑ Horseback   ❑
- ❑ Mountain Biking   ❑
- ❑ Watersports   ❑
- ❑ Wildlife   ❑
- ❑ Winter Sports

Facilities:

- ❑ ADA   ❑
- ❑ Gift Shop   ❑
- ❑ Museum   ❑
- ❑ Visitor Center   ❑
- ❑ Picnic sites   ❑
- ❑ Restrooms   ❑

Things to do in the area:

Get the Facts

- ❑ Phone   910-947-2051
- ❑ Park Hours

  _____

- ❑ Reservations? ____Y ____N

  date made_____

- ❑ Open all year? ____Y____N

  dates_____

- ❑ Dog friendly _____Y _____N

- ❑ Distance from home

  miles: _____

  hours: _____

- ❑ Address_____

  _____

  _____

Fees:

- ❑ Day Use $ _____
- ❑ Refund policy

  _____

  _____

  _____

Notes:

President James K. Polk Historic Site
City: Pineville   County: Mecklenburg

Plan your trip: https://historicsites.nc.gov/all-sites/president-james-k-polk

Activities:

- ❑ ATV / OHV   ❑
- ❑ Bike Trails   ❑
- ❑ Birding   ❑
- ❑ Boating   ❑
- ❑ Fishing   ❑
- ❑ Hiking   ❑
- ❑ Horseback   ❑
- ❑ Mountain Biking   ❑
- ❑ Watersports   ❑
- ❑ Wildlife   ❑
- ❑ Winter Sports

Facilities:

- ❑ ADA   ❑
- ❑ Gift Shop   ❑
- ❑ Museum   ❑
- ❑ Visitor Center   ❑
- ❑ Picnic sites   ❑
- ❑ Restrooms   ❑

Things to do in the area:

Get the Facts

- ❑ Phone   704-889-7145
- ❑ Park Hours

  _____

- ❑ Reservations? _____Y _____N

  date made_____

- ❑ Open all year? _____Y_____N

  dates_____

- ❑ Dog friendly _____Y _____N

- ❑ Distance from home

  miles: _____

  hours: _____

- ❑ Address_____

  _____

  _____

Fees:

- ❑ Day Use $ _____
- ❑ Refund policy

  _____

  _____

  _____

Notes:

Town Creek Indian Mound Historic Site
City: Gilead   County: Montgomery
Plan your trip: https://historicsites.nc.gov/node/69

Activities:

- [ ] ATV / OHV   [ ]
- [ ] Bike Trails   [ ]
- [ ] Birding   [ ]
- [ ] Boating   [ ]
- [ ] Fishing   [ ]
- [ ] Hiking   [ ]
- [ ] Horseback   [ ]
- [ ] Mountain Biking   [ ]
- [ ] Watersports   [ ]
- [ ] Wildlife   [ ]
- [ ] Winter Sports

Facilities:

- [ ] ADA   [ ]
- [ ] Gift Shop   [ ]
- [ ] Museum   [ ]
- [ ] Visitor Center   [ ]
- [ ] Picnic sites   [ ]
- [ ] Restrooms   [ ]

Things to do in the area:

Get the Facts

- [ ] Phone   910-439-6802
- [ ] Park Hours

  _____

- [ ] Reservations? _____Y _____N

  date made_____

- [ ] Open all year? _____Y_____N

  dates_____

- [ ] Dog friendly _____Y _____N

- [ ] Distance from home

  miles: _____

  hours: _____

- [ ] Address_____

  _____

  _____

Fees:

- [ ] Day Use $ _____
- [ ] Refund policy

  _____

  _____

  _____

Notes:

Weymouth Woods Sandhills Nature Preserve
City: Southern Pines   County: Moore

Plan your trip: https://www.ncparks.gov/weymouth-woods-sandhills-nature-preserve/home

Activities:

- ❑ ATV / OHV   ❑
- ❑ Bike Trails   ❑
- ❑ Birding   ❑
- ❑ Boating   ❑
- ❑ Fishing   ❑
- ❑ Hiking   ❑
- ❑ Horseback   ❑
- ❑ Mountain Biking   ❑
- ❑ Watersports   ❑
- ❑ Wildlife   ❑
- ❑ Winter Sports

Facilities:

- ❑ ADA   ❑
- ❑ Gift Shop   ❑
- ❑ Museum   ❑
- ❑ Visitor Center   ❑
- ❑ Picnic sites   ❑
- ❑ Restrooms   ❑

Things to do in the area:

Get the Facts

- ❑ Phone   910-692-2167
- ❑ Park Hours

  _____

- ❑ Reservations? ____Y ____N

  date made_____

- ❑ Open all year? ____Y____N

  dates_____

- ❑ Dog friendly _____Y _____N

- ❑ Distance from home

  miles: _____

  hours: _____

- ❑ Address_____

  _____

  _____

Fees:

- ❑ Day Use $ _____
- ❑ Refund policy

  _____

  _____

  _____

Notes:

Occoneechee Mountain State Natural Area
City: Hillsborough   County: Orange

Plan your trip: https://www.ncparks.gov/occoneechee-mountain-state-natural-area/home

Activities:

- ❏ ATV / OHV   ❏
- ❏ Bike Trails   ❏
- ❏ Birding   ❏
- ❏ Boating   ❏
- ❏ Fishing   ❏
- ❏ Hiking   ❏
- ❏ Horseback   ❏
- ❏ Mountain Biking   ❏
- ❏ Watersports   ❏
- ❏ Wildlife   ❏
- ❏ Winter Sports

Facilities:

- ❏ ADA   ❏
- ❏ Gift Shop   ❏
- ❏ Museum   ❏
- ❏ Visitor Center   ❏
- ❏ Picnic sites   ❏
- ❏ Restrooms   ❏

Things to do in the area:

Get the Facts

- ❏ Phone   919-383-1686
- ❏ Park Hours

  _____

- ❏ Reservations? ____Y ____N

  date made_____

- ❏ Open all year? ____Y____N

  dates_____

- ❏ Dog friendly _____Y _____N

- ❏ Distance from home

  miles: _____

  hours: _____

- ❏ Address_____

  _____

  _____

Fees:

- ❏ Day Use $ _____
- ❏ Refund policy

  _____

  _____

  _____

Notes:

North Carolina Transportation Museum
City: Spencer   County: Rowan

Plan your trip: https://www.nctrans.org/

Activities:

- ❏ ATV / OHV
- ❏ Bike Trails
- ❏ Birding
- ❏ Boating
- ❏ Fishing
- ❏ Hiking
- ❏ Horseback
- ❏ Mountain Biking
- ❏ Watersports
- ❏ Wildlife
- ❏ Winter Sports

- ❏
- ❏
- ❏
- ❏
- ❏
- ❏
- ❏
- ❏
- ❏
- ❏

Facilities:

- ❏ ADA
- ❏ Gift Shop
- ❏ Museum
- ❏ Visitor Center
- ❏ Picnic sites
- ❏ Restrooms

- ❏
- ❏
- ❏
- ❏
- ❏
- ❏

Things to do in the area:

Get the Facts

- ❏ Phone   704-636-2889
- ❏ Park Hours

  _____

- ❏ Reservations? _____Y _____N

  date made_____

- ❏ Open all year? _____Y_____N

  dates_____

- ❏ Dog friendly _____Y _____N

- ❏ Distance from home

  miles: _____

  hours: _____

- ❏ Address_____

  _____

  _____

Fees:

- ❏ Day Use $ _____
- ❏ Refund policy

  _____
  _____
  _____

Notes:

Horne Creek Farm Historic Site
City: Pinnacle   County: Stokes

Plan your trip: https://historicsites.nc.gov/node/60

Activities:

- [ ] ATV / OHV   [ ]
- [ ] Bike Trails   [ ]
- [ ] Birding   [ ]
- [ ] Boating   [ ]
- [ ] Fishing   [ ]
- [ ] Hiking   [ ]
- [ ] Horseback   [ ]
- [ ] Mountain Biking   [ ]
- [ ] Watersports   [ ]
- [ ] Wildlife   [ ]
- [ ] Winter Sports

Facilities:

- [ ] ADA   [ ]
- [ ] Gift Shop   [ ]
- [ ] Museum   [ ]
- [ ] Visitor Center   [ ]
- [ ] Picnic sites   [ ]
- [ ] Restrooms   [ ]

Things to do in the area:

Get the Facts

- [ ] Phone   336-325-2298
- [ ] Park Hours

_____

- [ ] Reservations? _____Y _____N

   date made_____

- [ ] Open all year? _____Y_____N

   dates_____

- [ ] Dog friendly _____Y _____N

- [ ] Distance from home

   miles: _____

   hours: _____

- [ ] Address_____

_____

_____

Fees:

- [ ] Day Use $ _____
- [ ] Refund policy

_____

_____

_____

Notes:

North Carolina State Capitol
City: Raleigh   County: Wake

Plan your trip: https://historicsites.nc.gov/node/67

Activities:

- ❑ ATV / OHV   ❑
- ❑ Bike Trails   ❑
- ❑ Birding   ❑
- ❑ Boating   ❑
- ❑ Fishing   ❑
- ❑ Hiking   ❑
- ❑ Horseback   ❑
- ❑ Mountain Biking   ❑
- ❑ Watersports   ❑
- ❑ Wildlife   ❑
- ❑ Winter Sports

Facilities:

- ❑ ADA   ❑
- ❑ Gift Shop   ❑
- ❑ Museum   ❑
- ❑ Visitor Center   ❑
- ❑ Picnic sites   ❑
- ❑ Restrooms   ❑

Things to do in the area:

Get the Facts

- ❑ Phone   919-733-4994
- ❑ Park Hours

  _____

- ❑ Reservations? ____Y ____N

  date made_____

- ❑ Open all year? ____Y____N

  dates_____

- ❑ Dog friendly _____Y _____N

- ❑ Distance from home

  miles: _____

  hours: _____

- ❑ Address_____

  _____

  _____

Fees:

- ❑ Day Use $ _____
- ❑ Refund policy

  _____

  _____

  _____

Notes:

Governor Charles B. Aycock Birthplace HS
City: Fremont   County: Wayne

Plan your trip: https://historicsites.nc.gov/node/46

Activities:

- ❑ ATV / OHV   ❑
- ❑ Bike Trails   ❑
- ❑ Birding   ❑
- ❑ Boating   ❑
- ❑ Fishing   ❑
- ❑ Hiking   ❑
- ❑ Horseback   ❑
- ❑ Mountain Biking   ❑
- ❑ Watersports   ❑
- ❑ Wildlife   ❑
- ❑ Winter Sports

Facilities:

- ❑ ADA   ❑
- ❑ Gift Shop   ❑
- ❑ Museum   ❑
- ❑ Visitor Center   ❑
- ❑ Picnic sites   ❑
- ❑ Restrooms   ❑

Things to do in the area:

Get the Facts

- ❑ Phone   919-242-5581
- ❑ Park Hours

  _____

- ❑ Reservations? _____Y _____N

  date made_____

- ❑ Open all year? _____Y_____N

  dates_____

- ❑ Dog friendly _____Y _____N

- ❑ Distance from home

  miles: _____

  hours: _____

- ❑ Address_____

  _____

  _____

Fees:

- ❑ Day Use $ _____
- ❑ Refund policy

  _____

  _____

  _____

Notes:

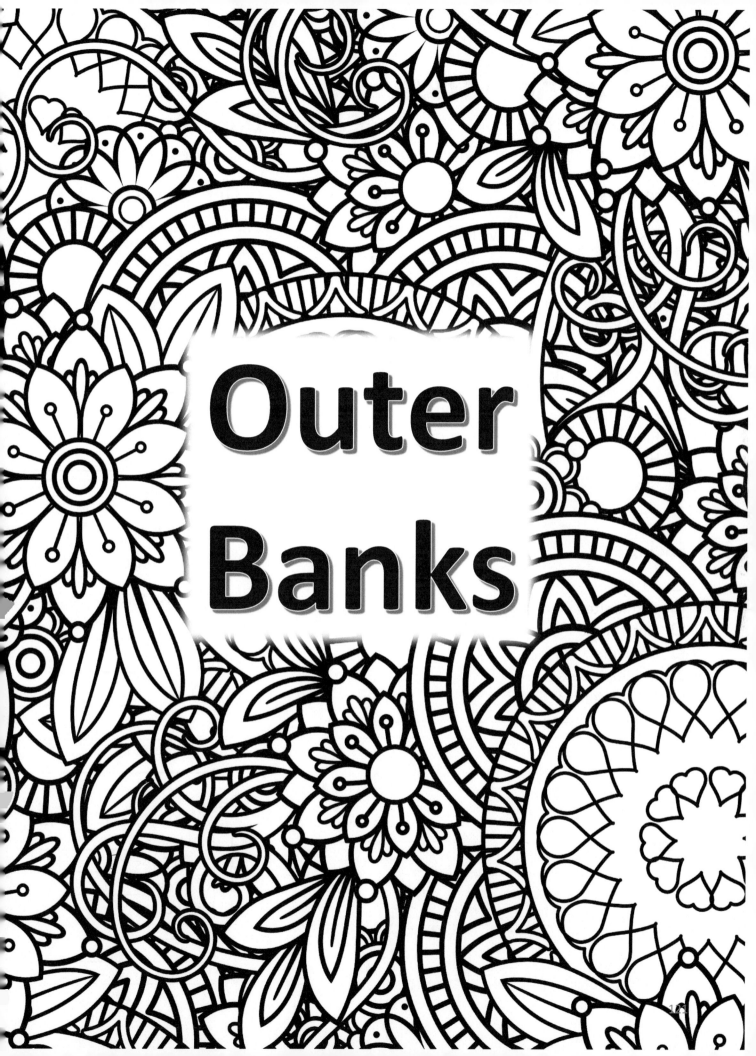

Rodanthe Beach
City: Rodanthe   County: Dare
Plan your trip: https://www.outerbanks.org/plan-your-trip/towns-and-villages/rodanthe/

Activities:

- ❑ Biking
- ❑ Boating
- ❑ Disc Golf
- ❑ Fishing
- ❑ Gold Panning
- ❑ Hiking
- ❑ Historic Learning
- ❑ Horseback Riding
- ❑ Hunting
- ❑ Kite Boarding

- ❑ Metal Detecting
- ❑ OHV
- ❑ Paddling
- ❑ Rock Climbing
- ❑ Stargazing
- ❑ Swimming
- ❑ Wildlife Viewing
- ❑ Windsurfing
- ❑
- ❑

- ❑
- ❑
- ❑
- ❑
- ❑
- ❑
- ❑
- ❑
- ❑
- ❑

Facilities:

- ❑ ADA
- ❑ Picnic sites
- ❑ Restrooms
- ❑ Showers
- ❑ Trailer Access
- ❑ Visitor center
- ❑ Group Camping
- ❑ RV Camp
- ❑ Rustic Camping
- ❑ Cabins / Yurts
- ❑ Day Use Area

Notes:

Get the Facts

- ❑ Phone   877-629-4386
- ❑ Park Hours

  _____

- ❑ Reservations? ____Y ____N

  date made_____
- ❑ Open all year ____Y____N

  dates_____
- ❑ Check in time _____
- ❑ Check out time _____
- ❑ Pet friendly _____Y _____N
- ❑ Max RV length _____
- ❑ Distance from home

  miles: _____

  hours: _____
- ❑ Address_____

  _____

  _____

Fees:

- ❑ Day Use $ _____
- ❑ Camp Sites $ _____
- ❑ RV Sites $ _____
- ❑ Refund policy

  _____

  _____

  _____

Make It Personal

Trip dates: _____

The weather was: Sunny Cloudy Rainy Stormy Snowy Foggy Warm Cold

Why I went: _____

How I got there: (circle all that apply)   Plane   Train   Car   Bus   Bike   Hike   RV   MC

I went with: _____

We stayed in (space, cabin # etc): _____

Most relaxing day: _____

Something funny: _____

Someone we met: _____

Best story told: _____

The kids liked this: _____

The best food: _____

Games played: _____

Something disappointing: _____

Next time I'll do this differently: _____

Waves Beach

City: Waves   County: Dare

Plan your trip: https://www.outerbanks.org/plan-your-trip/towns-and-villages/waves/

Activities:

- ☐ Biking
- ☐ Boating
- ☐ Disc Golf
- ☐ Fishing
- ☐ Gold Panning
- ☐ Hiking
- ☐ Historic Learning
- ☐ Horseback Riding
- ☐ Hunting
- ☐ Kite Boarding
- ☐ Metal Detecting
- ☐ OHV
- ☐ Paddling
- ☐ Rock Climbing
- ☐ Stargazing
- ☐ Swimming
- ☐ Wildlife Viewing
- ☐ Windsurfing

Facilities:

- ☐ ADA
- ☐ Picnic sites
- ☐ Restrooms
- ☐ Showers
- ☐ Trailer Access
- ☐ Visitor center
- ☐ Group Camping
- ☐ RV Camp
- ☐ Rustic Camping
- ☐ Cabins / Yurts
- ☐ Day Use Area

Notes:

Get the Facts

- ☐ Phone   877-629-4386
- ☐ Park Hours

  _____

- ☐ Reservations? ____Y ____N

  date made_____
- ☐ Open all year ____Y____N

  dates_____
- ☐ Check in time _____
- ☐ Check out time _____
- ☐ Pet friendly _____Y _____N
- ☐ Max RV length _____
- ☐ Distance from home

  miles: _____

  hours: _____
- ☐ Address_____

  _____

  _____

Fees:

- ☐ Day Use $ _____
- ☐ Camp Sites $ _____
- ☐ RV Sites $ _____
- ☐ Refund policy

  _____

  _____

  _____

Make It Personal

Trip dates:

The weather was: Sunny Cloudy Rainy Stormy Snowy Foggy Warm Cold

Why I went:

How I got there: (circle all that apply) Plane Train Car Bus Bike Hike RV MC

I went with:

We stayed in (space, cabin # etc):

Most relaxing day:

Something funny:

Someone we met:

Best story told:

The kids liked this:

The best food:

Games played:

Something disappointing:

Next time I'll do this differently:

Buxton Beach

City: Buxton   County: Dare

Plan your trip: https://www.outerbanks.org/plan-your-trip/towns-and-villages/buxton/

Activities:

- ☐ Biking
- ☐ Boating
- ☐ Disc Golf
- ☐ Fishing
- ☐ Gold Panning
- ☐ Hiking
- ☐ Historic Learning
- ☐ Horseback Riding
- ☐ Hunting
- ☐ Kite Boarding

- ☐ Metal Detecting
- ☐ OHV
- ☐ Paddling
- ☐ Rock Climbing
- ☐ Stargazing
- ☐ Swimming
- ☐ Wildlife Viewing
- ☐ Windsurfing
- ☐
- ☐

- ☐
- ☐
- ☐
- ☐
- ☐
- ☐
- ☐
- ☐
- ☐
- ☐

Facilities:

- ☐ ADA
- ☐ Picnic sites
- ☐ Restrooms
- ☐ Showers
- ☐ Trailer Access
- ☐ Visitor center
- ☐ Group Camping
- ☐ RV Camp
- ☐ Rustic Camping
- ☐ Cabins / Yurts
- ☐ Day Use Area

Notes:

Get the Facts

- ☐ Phone   877-629-4386
- ☐ Park Hours

    _____

- ☐ Reservations? _____Y _____N

    date made_____

- ☐ Open all year _____Y_____N

    dates_____

- ☐ Check in time _____
- ☐ Check out time _____
- ☐ Pet friendly _____Y _____N
- ☐ Max RV length _____
- ☐ Distance from home

    miles: _____

    hours: _____

- ☐ Address_____

    _____

    _____

Fees:

- ☐ Day Use $ _____
- ☐ Camp Sites $ _____
- ☐ RV Sites $ _____
- ☐ Refund policy

    _____

    _____

    _____

Make It Personal

Trip dates:

The weather was: Sunny Cloudy Rainy Stormy Snowy Foggy Warm Cold

Why I went:

How I got there: (circle all that apply) Plane Train Car Bus Bike Hike RV MC

I went with:

We stayed in (space, cabin # etc):

Most relaxing day:

Something funny:

Someone we met:

Best story told:

The kids liked this:

The best food:

Games played:

Something disappointing:

Next time I'll do this differently:

Frisco Beach
City: Frisco   County: Dare
Plan your trip: https://www.outerbanks.org/plan-your-trip/towns-and-villages/frisco/

Activities:

- ❑ Biking
- ❑ Boating
- ❑ Disc Golf
- ❑ Fishing
- ❑ Gold Panning
- ❑ Hiking
- ❑ Historic Learning
- ❑ Horseback Riding
- ❑ Hunting
- ❑ Kite Boarding

- ❑ Metal Detecting
- ❑ OHV
- ❑ Paddling
- ❑ Rock Climbing
- ❑ Stargazing
- ❑ Swimming
- ❑ Wildlife Viewing
- ❑ Windsurfing
- ❑
- ❑

- ❑
- ❑
- ❑
- ❑
- ❑
- ❑
- ❑
- ❑
- ❑
- ❑

Facilities:

- ❑ ADA
- ❑ Picnic sites
- ❑ Restrooms
- ❑ Showers
- ❑ Trailer Access
- ❑ Visitor center
- ❑ Group Camping
- ❑ RV Camp
- ❑ Rustic Camping
- ❑ Cabins / Yurts
- ❑ Day Use Area

Notes:

Get the Facts

- ❑ Phone   877-629-4386
- ❑ Park Hours

  _____

- ❑ Reservations? ____Y ____N

  date made_____

- ❑ Open all year ____Y____N

  dates_____

- ❑ Check in time _____

- ❑ Check out time _____

- ❑ Pet friendly _____Y _____N

- ❑ Max RV length _____

- ❑ Distance from home

  miles: _____

  hours: _____

- ❑ Address_____

  _____

  _____

Fees:

- ❑ Day Use $ _____
- ❑ Camp Sites $ _____
- ❑ RV Sites $ _____
- ❑ Refund policy

  _____

  _____

  _____

Make It Personal

Trip dates: _____ | The weather was: Sunny Cloudy Rainy Stormy Snowy Foggy Warm Cold

Why I went:
_____

_____

How I got there: (circle all that apply) Plane Train Car Bus Bike Hike RV MC
_____

I went with:
_____

We stayed in (space, cabin # etc):
_____

Most relaxing day:
_____

_____

Something funny:
_____

_____

Someone we met:
_____

_____

Best story told:
_____

_____

The kids liked this:
_____

_____

The best food:
_____

_____

Games played:
_____

_____

Something disappointing:
_____

_____

Next time I'll do this differently:
_____

_____

Ocracoke Beach
City: Ocracoke   County: Hyde

Plan your trip: https://www.visitocracokenc.com/about-the-area/beaches-wildlife/

Activities:

- ❑ Biking
- ❑ Boating
- ❑ Disc Golf
- ❑ Fishing
- ❑ Gold Panning
- ❑ Hiking
- ❑ Historic Learning
- ❑ Horseback Riding
- ❑ Hunting
- ❑ Kite Boarding

- ❑ Metal Detecting
- ❑ OHV
- ❑ Paddling
- ❑ Rock Climbing
- ❑ Stargazing
- ❑ Swimming
- ❑ Wildlife Viewing
- ❑ Windsurfing
- ❑
- ❑

- ❑
- ❑
- ❑
- ❑
- ❑
- ❑
- ❑
- ❑
- ❑
- ❑

Facilities:

- ❑ ADA
- ❑ Picnic sites
- ❑ Restrooms
- ❑ Showers
- ❑ Trailer Access
- ❑ Visitor center
- ❑ Group Camping
- ❑ RV Camp
- ❑ Rustic Camping
- ❑ Cabins / Yurts
- ❑ Day Use Area

Notes:

Get the Facts

- ❑ Phone   252-928-6711
- ❑ Park Hours

  _____

- ❑ Reservations? ____Y ____N

  date made_____

- ❑ Open all year ____Y____N

  dates_____

- ❑ Check in time _____

- ❑ Check out time _____

- ❑ Pet friendly _____Y _____N

- ❑ Max RV length _____

- ❑ Distance from home

  miles: _____

  hours: _____

- ❑ Address_____

  _____

  _____

Fees:

- ❑ Day Use $ _____
- ❑ Camp Sites $ _____
- ❑ RV Sites $ _____
- ❑ Refund policy

  _____

  _____

  _____

Make It Personal

Trip dates:

The weather was: Sunny Cloudy Rainy Stormy Snowy Foggy Warm Cold

Why I went:

How I got there: (circle all that apply) Plane Train Car Bus Bike Hike RV MC

I went with:

We stayed in (space, cabin # etc):

Most relaxing day:

Something funny:

Someone we met:

Best story told:

The kids liked this:

The best food:

Games played:

Something disappointing:

Next time I'll do this differently:

Carova Beach

City: Carvova   County: Currituck

Plan your trip: https://www.outerbanks.com/carova.html

Activities:

- [ ] ATV / OHV   [ ]
- [ ] Bike Trails   [ ]
- [ ] Birding   [ ]
- [ ] Boating   [ ]
- [ ] Fishing   [ ]
- [ ] Hiking   [ ]
- [ ] Horseback   [ ]
- [ ] Mountain Biking   [ ]
- [ ] Watersports   [ ]
- [ ] Wildlife   [ ]
- [ ] Winter Sports

Facilities:

- [ ] ADA   [ ]
- [ ] Gift Shop   [ ]
- [ ] Museum   [ ]
- [ ] Visitor Center   [ ]
- [ ] Picnic sites   [ ]
- [ ] Restrooms   [ ]

Things to do in the area:

Get the Facts

- [ ] Phone
- [ ] Park Hours

_____

- [ ] Reservations? ____Y ____N

date made_____

- [ ] Open all year? ____Y____N

dates_____

- [ ] Dog friendly _____Y _____N
- [ ] Distance from home

miles: _____

hours: _____

- [ ] Address_____

_____

_____

Fees:

- [ ] Day Use $ _____
- [ ] Refund policy

_____

_____

_____

Notes:

Currituck National Wildlife Refuge
City: Corolla   County: Currituck

Plan your trip: https://www.fws.gov/refuge/Currituck/

Activities:

- ❑ ATV / OHV ❑
- ❑ Bike Trails ❑
- ❑ Birding ❑
- ❑ Boating ❑
- ❑ Fishing ❑
- ❑ Hiking ❑
- ❑ Horseback ❑
- ❑ Mountain Biking ❑
- ❑ Watersports ❑
- ❑ Wildlife ❑
- ❑ Winter Sports

Facilities:

- ❑ ADA ❑
- ❑ Gift Shop ❑
- ❑ Museum ❑
- ❑ Visitor Center ❑
- ❑ Picnic sites ❑
- ❑ Restrooms ❑

Things to do in the area:

Get the Facts

- ❑ Phone
- ❑ Park Hours

  _____

- ❑ Reservations? ____Y ____N

  date made_____

- ❑ Open all year? ____Y____N

  dates_____

- ❑ Dog friendly _____Y _____N

- ❑ Distance from home

  miles: _____

  hours: _____

- ❑ Address_____

  _____

  _____

Fees:

- ❑ Day Use $ _____
- ❑ Refund policy

  _____

  _____

  _____

Notes:

Currituck Beach Lighthouse
City: Corolla   County: Currituck

Plan your trip: https://obcinc.org/

Activities:

- ❑ ATV / OHV   ❑
- ❑ Bike Trails   ❑
- ❑ Birding   ❑
- ❑ Boating   ❑
- ❑ Fishing   ❑
- ❑ Hiking   ❑
- ❑ Horseback   ❑
- ❑ Mountain Biking   ❑
- ❑ Watersports   ❑
- ❑ Wildlife   ❑
- ❑ Winter Sports

Facilities:

- ❑ ADA   ❑
- ❑ Gift Shop   ❑
- ❑ Museum   ❑
- ❑ Visitor Center   ❑
- ❑ Picnic sites   ❑
- ❑ Restrooms   ❑

Things to do in the area:

Get the Facts

- ❑ Phone   252-453-4939
- ❑ Park Hours

  _____

- ❑ Reservations? ____Y ____N

  date made_____
- ❑ Open all year? ____Y____N

  dates_____
- ❑ Dog friendly _____Y _____N
- ❑ Distance from home

  miles: _____

  hours: _____
- ❑ Address_____

  _____

  _____

Fees:

- ❑ Day Use $ _____
- ❑ Refund policy

  _____

  _____

  _____

Notes:

134

Corolla Beach
City: Corolla   County: Currituck
Plan your trip: https://www.outerbanks.com/corolla.html

Activities:

- ❑ ATV / OHV   ❑
- ❑ Bike Trails   ❑
- ❑ Birding   ❑
- ❑ Boating   ❑
- ❑ Fishing   ❑
- ❑ Hiking   ❑
- ❑ Horseback   ❑
- ❑ Mountain Biking   ❑
- ❑ Watersports   ❑
- ❑ Wildlife   ❑
- ❑ Winter Sports

Facilities:

- ❑ ADA   ❑
- ❑ Gift Shop   ❑
- ❑ Museum   ❑
- ❑ Visitor Center   ❑
- ❑ Picnic sites   ❑
- ❑ Restrooms   ❑

Things to do in the area:

Get the Facts

- ❑ Phone
- ❑ Park Hours

_____

- ❑ Reservations? ____Y ____N

  date made_____

- ❑ Open all year? ____Y____N

  dates_____

- ❑ Dog friendly _____Y _____N

- ❑ Distance from home

  miles: _____

  hours: _____

- ❑ Address_____

  _____

  _____

Fees:

- ❑ Day Use $ _____
- ❑ Refund policy

  _____

  _____

  _____

Notes:

Duck Beach
City: Duck   County: Dare

Plan your trip: https://www.outerbanks.org/plan-your-trip/towns-and-villages/duck/

Activities:

- ❑ ATV / OHV   ❑
- ❑ Bike Trails   ❑
- ❑ Birding   ❑
- ❑ Boating   ❑
- ❑ Fishing   ❑
- ❑ Hiking   ❑
- ❑ Horseback   ❑
- ❑ Mountain Biking   ❑
- ❑ Watersports   ❑
- ❑ Wildlife   ❑
- ❑ Winter Sports

Facilities:

- ❑ ADA   ❑
- ❑ Gift Shop   ❑
- ❑ Museum   ❑
- ❑ Visitor Center   ❑
- ❑ Picnic sites   ❑
- ❑ Restrooms   ❑

Things to do in the area:

Get the Facts

- ❑ Phone   877-629-4386
- ❑ Park Hours

  _____

- ❑ Reservations? ____Y ____N

  date made_____

- ❑ Open all year? ____Y____N

  dates_____

- ❑ Dog friendly _____Y _____N

- ❑ Distance from home

  miles: _____

  hours: _____

- ❑ Address_____

  _____

  _____

Fees:

- ❑ Day Use $ _____
- ❑ Refund policy

  _____

  _____

  _____

Notes:

Southern Shores Beach
City: Southern Shores   County: Dare

Plan your trip: https://www.outerbanks.org/plan-your-trip/towns-and-villages/southern-shores/

Activities:

- ❑ ATV / OHV   ❑
- ❑ Bike Trails   ❑
- ❑ Birding   ❑
- ❑ Boating   ❑
- ❑ Fishing   ❑
- ❑ Hiking   ❑
- ❑ Horseback   ❑
- ❑ Mountain Biking   ❑
- ❑ Watersports   ❑
- ❑ Wildlife   ❑
- ❑ Winter Sports

Facilities:

- ❑ ADA   ❑
- ❑ Gift Shop   ❑
- ❑ Museum   ❑
- ❑ Visitor Center   ❑
- ❑ Picnic sites   ❑
- ❑ Restrooms   ❑

Things to do in the area:

Get the Facts

- ❑ Phone   877-629-4386
- ❑ Park Hours

  _____

- ❑ Reservations? ____Y ____N

  date made_____

- ❑ Open all year? ____Y____N

  dates_____

- ❑ Dog friendly _____Y _____N

- ❑ Distance from home

  miles: _____

  hours: _____

- ❑ Address_____

  _____

  _____

Fees:

- ❑ Day Use $ _____
- ❑ Refund policy

  _____

  _____

  _____

Notes:

Kitty Hawk Woods Coastal Reserve
City: Kitty Hawk   County: Dare

Plan your trip: https://www.outerbanks.org/plan-your-trip/towns-and-villages/kitty-hawk/

Activities:

- ❑ ATV / OHV   ❑
- ❑ Bike Trails   ❑
- ❑ Birding   ❑
- ❑ Boating   ❑
- ❑ Fishing   ❑
- ❑ Hiking   ❑
- ❑ Horseback   ❑
- ❑ Mountain Biking   ❑
- ❑ Watersports   ❑
- ❑ Wildlife   ❑
- ❑ Winter Sports

Facilities:

- ❑ ADA   ❑
- ❑ Gift Shop   ❑
- ❑ Museum   ❑
- ❑ Visitor Center   ❑
- ❑ Picnic sites   ❑
- ❑ Restrooms   ❑

Things to do in the area:

Get the Facts

- ❑ Phone   877-629-4386
- ❑ Park Hours

  _____

- ❑ Reservations? ـــــــY ـــــــN

  date made_____

- ❑ Open all year? ـــــــYـــــــN

  dates_____

- ❑ Dog friendly ـــــــY ـــــــN

- ❑ Distance from home

  miles: _____

  hours: _____

- ❑ Address_____

  _____

  _____

Fees:

- ❑ Day Use $ _____
- ❑ Refund policy

  _____

  _____

  _____

Notes:

Kill Devil Hills
City: Kill Devil Hills   County: Dare

Plan your trip: https://www.outerbanks.org/plan-your-trip/towns-and-villages/kill-devil-hills/

Activities:

- ❑ ATV / OHV   ❑
- ❑ Bike Trails   ❑
- ❑ Birding   ❑
- ❑ Boating   ❑
- ❑ Fishing   ❑
- ❑ Hiking   ❑
- ❑ Horseback   ❑
- ❑ Mountain Biking   ❑
- ❑ Watersports   ❑
- ❑ Wildlife   ❑
- ❑ Winter Sports

Facilities:

- ❑ ADA   ❑
- ❑ Gift Shop   ❑
- ❑ Museum   ❑
- ❑ Visitor Center   ❑
- ❑ Picnic sites   ❑
- ❑ Restrooms   ❑

Things to do in the area:

Get the Facts

- ❑ Phone   877-629-4386
- ❑ Park Hours

  _____

- ❑ Reservations? _____Y _____N

  date made_____

- ❑ Open all year? _____Y_____N

  dates_____

- ❑ Dog friendly _____Y _____N

- ❑ Distance from home

  miles: _____

  hours: _____

- ❑ Address_____

  _____

  _____

Fees:

- ❑ Day Use $ _____
- ❑ Refund policy

  _____

  _____

  _____

Notes:

Nags Head Beach
City: Nags Head   County: Dare
Plan your trip: https://www.outerbanks.org/plan-your-trip/towns-and-villages/nags-head/

Activities:

- ❑ ATV / OHV ❑
- ❑ Bike Trails ❑
- ❑ Birding ❑
- ❑ Boating ❑
- ❑ Fishing ❑
- ❑ Hiking ❑
- ❑ Horseback ❑
- ❑ Mountain Biking ❑
- ❑ Watersports ❑
- ❑ Wildlife ❑
- ❑ Winter Sports

Facilities:

- ❑ ADA ❑
- ❑ Gift Shop ❑
- ❑ Museum ❑
- ❑ Visitor Center ❑
- ❑ Picnic sites ❑
- ❑ Restrooms ❑

Things to do in the area:

Get the Facts

- ❑ Phone   877-629-4386
- ❑ Park Hours

_____

- ❑ Reservations? ____Y ____N

date made_____

- ❑ Open all year? ____Y____N

dates_____

- ❑ Dog friendly _____Y _____N
- ❑ Distance from home

miles: _____

hours: _____

- ❑ Address_____

_____

_____

Fees:

- ❑ Day Use $ _____
- ❑ Refund policy

_____

_____

_____

Notes:

Manteo Island

City: Manteo   County: Dare

Plan your trip: https://www.outerbanks.org/plan-your-trip/towns-and-villages/manteo/

Activities:

- ❑ ATV / OHV
- ❑ Bike Trails
- ❑ Birding
- ❑ Boating
- ❑ Fishing
- ❑ Hiking
- ❑ Horseback
- ❑ Mountain Biking
- ❑ Watersports
- ❑ Wildlife
- ❑ Winter Sports

- ❑
- ❑
- ❑
- ❑
- ❑
- ❑
- ❑
- ❑
- ❑
- ❑

Facilities:

- ❑ ADA
- ❑ Gift Shop
- ❑ Museum
- ❑ Visitor Center
- ❑ Picnic sites
- ❑ Restrooms

- ❑
- ❑
- ❑
- ❑
- ❑
- ❑

Things to do in the area:

Get the Facts

- ❑ Phone   877-629-4386
- ❑ Park Hours

  _____

- ❑ Reservations? ____Y ____N

  date made_____

- ❑ Open all year? ____Y____N

  dates_____

- ❑ Dog friendly _____Y _____N

- ❑ Distance from home

  miles: _____

  hours: _____

- ❑ Address_____

  _____

  _____

Fees:

- ❑ Day Use $ _____
- ❑ Refund policy

  _____
  _____
  _____

Notes:

141

Wanchese Island
City: Wanchese   County: Dare
Plan your trip: https://www.outerbanks.org/plan-your-trip/towns-and-villages/wanchese/

Activities:

- ❏ ATV / OHV   ❏
- ❏ Bike Trails   ❏
- ❏ Birding   ❏
- ❏ Boating   ❏
- ❏ Fishing   ❏
- ❏ Hiking   ❏
- ❏ Horseback   ❏
- ❏ Mountain Biking   ❏
- ❏ Watersports   ❏
- ❏ Wildlife   ❏
- ❏ Winter Sports

Facilities:

- ❏ ADA   ❏
- ❏ Gift Shop   ❏
- ❏ Museum   ❏
- ❏ Visitor Center   ❏
- ❏ Picnic sites   ❏
- ❏ Restrooms   ❏

Things to do in the area:

Get the Facts

- ❏ Phone   877-629-4386
- ❏ Park Hours

  _____

- ❏ Reservations? _____Y _____N

  date made_____

- ❏ Open all year? _____Y_____N

  dates_____

- ❏ Dog friendly _____Y _____N

- ❏ Distance from home

  miles: _____

  hours: _____

- ❏ Address_____

  _____

  _____

Fees:

- ❏ Day Use $ _____
- ❏ Refund policy

  _____

  _____

  _____

Notes:

Cape Hatteras National Seashore
City: Nags Head   County: Dare

Plan your trip: https://www.stateparks.com/cape_hatteras_state_park_in_north_carolina.html

Activities:

- ❏ ATV / OHV   ❏
- ❏ Bike Trails   ❏
- ❏ Birding   ❏
- ❏ Boating   ❏
- ❏ Fishing   ❏
- ❏ Hiking   ❏
- ❏ Horseback   ❏
- ❏ Mountain Biking   ❏
- ❏ Watersports   ❏
- ❏ Wildlife   ❏
- ❏ Winter Sports

Facilities:

- ❏ ADA   ❏
- ❏ Gift Shop   ❏
- ❏ Museum   ❏
- ❏ Visitor Center   ❏
- ❏ Picnic sites   ❏
- ❏ Restrooms   ❏

Things to do in the area:

Get the Facts

- ❏ Phone 252-473-2111
- ❏ Park Hours

  _____

- ❏ Reservations? _____Y _____N

  date made_____

- ❏ Open all year? _____Y_____N

  dates_____

- ❏ Dog friendly _____Y _____N

- ❏ Distance from home

  miles: _____

  hours: _____

- ❏ Address_____

  _____

  _____

Fees:

- ❏ Day Use $ _____
- ❏ Refund policy

  _____

  _____

  _____

Notes:

Bodie Island Lighthouse
City: Nags Head   County: Dare

Plan your trip: https://www.nps.gov/caha/planyourvisit/bils.htm

Activities:

- ❑ ATV / OHV   ❑
- ❑ Bike Trails   ❑
- ❑ Birding   ❑
- ❑ Boating   ❑
- ❑ Fishing   ❑
- ❑ Hiking   ❑
- ❑ Horseback   ❑
- ❑ Mountain Biking   ❑
- ❑ Watersports   ❑
- ❑ Wildlife   ❑
- ❑ Winter Sports

Facilities:

- ❑ ADA   ❑
- ❑ Gift Shop   ❑
- ❑ Museum   ❑
- ❑ Visitor Center   ❑
- ❑ Picnic sites   ❑
- ❑ Restrooms   ❑

Things to do in the area:

Get the Facts

- ❑ Phone 252-473-2111
- ❑ Park Hours

  _____

- ❑ Reservations? ____Y ____N

  date made_____

- ❑ Open all year? ____Y____N

  dates_____

- ❑ Dog friendly _____Y _____N

- ❑ Distance from home

  miles: _____

  hours: _____

- ❑ Address_____

  _____

  _____

Fees:

- ❑ Day Use $ _____
- ❑ Refund policy

  _____

  _____

  _____

Notes:

Pea Island National Wildlife Refuge

City: Rodanthe   **County: Dare**

Plan your trip: https://www.outerbanks.com/pea-island-national-wildlife-refuge.html

Activities:

- ❑ ATV / OHV   ❑
- ❑ Bike Trails   ❑
- ❑ Birding   ❑
- ❑ Boating   ❑
- ❑ Fishing   ❑
- ❑ Hiking   ❑
- ❑ Horseback   ❑
- ❑ Mountain Biking   ❑
- ❑ Watersports   ❑
- ❑ Wildlife   ❑
- ❑ Winter Sports

Facilities:

- ❑ ADA   ❑
- ❑ Gift Shop   ❑
- ❑ Museum   ❑
- ❑ Visitor Center   ❑
- ❑ Picnic sites   ❑
- ❑ Restrooms   ❑

Things to do in the area:

Get the Facts

- ❑ Phone 252-473-1131
- ❑ Park Hours

  _____

- ❑ Reservations? ____Y ____N

  date made_____

- ❑ Open all year? ____Y____N

  dates_____

- ❑ Dog friendly _____Y _____N

- ❑ Distance from home

  miles: _____

  hours: _____

- ❑ Address_____

  _____

  _____

Fees:

- ❑ Day Use $ _____
- ❑ Refund policy

  _____

  _____

  _____

Notes:

Salvo Day Use Area
City: Waves   County: Dare
Plan your trip: https://www.outerbanks.org/plan-your-trip/towns-and-villages/salvo/

Activities:

- [ ] ATV / OHV   [ ]
- [ ] Bike Trails   [ ]
- [ ] Birding   [ ]
- [ ] Boating   [ ]
- [ ] Fishing   [ ]
- [ ] Hiking   [ ]
- [ ] Horseback   [ ]
- [ ] Mountain Biking   [ ]
- [ ] Watersports   [ ]
- [ ] Wildlife   [ ]
- [ ] Winter Sports

Facilities:

- [ ] ADA   [ ]
- [ ] Gift Shop   [ ]
- [ ] Museum   [ ]
- [ ] Visitor Center   [ ]
- [ ] Picnic sites   [ ]
- [ ] Restrooms   [ ]

Things to do in the area:

Get the Facts

- [ ] Phone   877-629-4386
- [ ] Park Hours

  _____

- [ ] Reservations? ____Y ____N

  date made_____

- [ ] Open all year? ____Y____N

  dates_____

- [ ] Dog friendly _____Y _____N

- [ ] Distance from home

  miles: _____

  hours: _____

- [ ] Address_____

  _____

  _____

Fees:

- [ ] Day Use $ _____
- [ ] Refund policy

  _____

  _____

  _____

Notes:

Avon Beach

City: Avon

County: Dare

Plan your trip: https://www.outerbanks.org/plan-your-trip/towns-and-villages/avon/

Activities:

- ❑ ATV / OHV
- ❑ Bike Trails
- ❑ Birding
- ❑ Boating
- ❑ Fishing
- ❑ Hiking
- ❑ Horseback
- ❑ Mountain Biking
- ❑ Watersports
- ❑ Wildlife
- ❑ Winter Sports

- ❑
- ❑
- ❑
- ❑
- ❑
- ❑
- ❑
- ❑
- ❑
- ❑

Facilities:

- ❑ ADA
- ❑ Gift Shop
- ❑ Museum
- ❑ Visitor Center
- ❑ Picnic sites
- ❑ Restrooms

- ❑
- ❑
- ❑
- ❑
- ❑
- ❑

Things to do in the area:

Get the Facts

- ❑ Phone   877-629-4386
- ❑ Park Hours

  _____

- ❑ Reservations? ____Y ____N

  date made_____

- ❑ Open all year? ____Y____N

  dates_____

- ❑ Dog friendly _____Y _____N

- ❑ Distance from home

  miles: _____

  hours: _____

- ❑ Address_____

  _____

  _____

Fees:

- ❑ Day Use $ _____
- ❑ Refund policy

  _____

  _____

  _____

Notes:

147

Cape Hatteras Lighthouse
City: Buxton   County: Dare

Plan your trip: https://www.nps.gov/caha/planyourvisit/chls.htm

Activities:

- ❑ ATV / OHV   ❑
- ❑ Bike Trails   ❑
- ❑ Birding   ❑
- ❑ Boating   ❑
- ❑ Fishing   ❑
- ❑ Hiking   ❑
- ❑ Horseback   ❑
- ❑ Mountain Biking   ❑
- ❑ Watersports   ❑
- ❑ Wildlife   ❑
- ❑ Winter Sports

Facilities:

- ❑ ADA   ❑
- ❑ Gift Shop   ❑
- ❑ Museum   ❑
- ❑ Visitor Center   ❑
- ❑ Picnic sites   ❑
- ❑ Restrooms   ❑

Things to do in the area:

Get the Facts

- ❑ Phone 252-473-2111
- ❑ Park Hours

  _____

- ❑ Reservations? ____Y ____N

  date made_____

- ❑ Open all year? ____Y____N

  dates_____

- ❑ Dog friendly _____Y _____N

- ❑ Distance from home

  miles: _____

  hours: _____

- ❑ Address_____

  _____

  _____

Fees:

- ❑ Day Use $ _____
- ❑ Refund policy

  _____

  _____

  _____

Notes:

Hatteras Beach
City: Hatteras   County: Dare
Plan your trip: https://www.outerbanks.org/plan-your-trip/towns-and-villages/hatteras/

Activities:

- ❑ ATV / OHV
- ❑ Bike Trails
- ❑ Birding
- ❑ Boating
- ❑ Fishing
- ❑ Hiking
- ❑ Horseback
- ❑ Mountain Biking
- ❑ Watersports
- ❑ Wildlife
- ❑ Winter Sports

❑ ❑ ❑ ❑ ❑ ❑ ❑ ❑ ❑ ❑

Facilities:

- ❑ ADA
- ❑ Gift Shop
- ❑ Museum
- ❑ Visitor Center
- ❑ Picnic sites
- ❑ Restrooms

❑ ❑ ❑ ❑ ❑ ❑

Things to do in the area:

Get the Facts

- ❑ Phone   877-629-4386
- ❑ Park Hours

_____

- ❑ Reservations? ____Y ____N

date made_____

- ❑ Open all year? ____Y____N

dates_____

- ❑ Dog friendly _____Y _____N

- ❑ Distance from home

miles: _____

hours: _____

- ❑ Address_____

_____

_____

Fees:

- ❑ Day Use $ _____
- ❑ Refund policy

_____

_____

_____

Notes:

Ocracoke Lighthouse
City: Ocracoke   County: Hyde

Plan your trip: https://www.nps.gov/caha/planyourvisit/ols.htm

Activities:

- ❑ ATV / OHV   ❑
- ❑ Bike Trails   ❑
- ❑ Birding   ❑
- ❑ Boating   ❑
- ❑ Fishing   ❑
- ❑ Hiking   ❑
- ❑ Horseback   ❑
- ❑ Mountain Biking   ❑
- ❑ Watersports   ❑
- ❑ Wildlife   ❑
- ❑ Winter Sports

Facilities:

- ❑ ADA   ❑
- ❑ Gift Shop   ❑
- ❑ Museum   ❑
- ❑ Visitor Center   ❑
- ❑ Picnic sites   ❑
- ❑ Restrooms   ❑

Things to do in the area:

Get the Facts

- ❑ Phone   252-473-2111
- ❑ Park Hours

  _____

- ❑ Reservations? ____Y ____N

  date made_____

- ❑ Open all year? ____Y____N

  dates_____

- ❑ Dog friendly _____Y _____N

- ❑ Distance from home

  miles: _____

  hours: _____

- ❑ Address_____

  _____

  _____

Fees:

- ❑ Day Use $ _____
- ❑ Refund policy

  _____

  _____

  _____

Notes:

150

Portsmouth Island

City: Portsmouth

County: Carteret

Plan your trip: https://www.outerbanks.com/portsmouth-island.html

Activities:

- ❑ ATV / OHV ❑
- ❑ Bike Trails ❑
- ❑ Birding ❑
- ❑ Boating ❑
- ❑ Fishing ❑
- ❑ Hiking ❑
- ❑ Horseback ❑
- ❑ Mountain Biking ❑
- ❑ Watersports ❑
- ❑ Wildlife ❑
- ❑ Winter Sports

Facilities:

- ❑ ADA ❑
- ❑ Gift Shop ❑
- ❑ Museum ❑
- ❑ Visitor Center ❑
- ❑ Picnic sites ❑
- ❑ Restrooms ❑

Things to do in the area:

Get the Facts

- ❑ Phone
- ❑ Park Hours

  _____

- ❑ Reservations? ____Y ____N

  date made_____

- ❑ Open all year? ____Y____N

  dates_____

- ❑ Dog friendly _____Y _____N

- ❑ Distance from home

  miles: _____

  hours: _____

- ❑ Address_____

  _____

  _____

Fees:

- ❑ Day Use $ _____
- ❑ Refund policy

  _____

  _____

  _____

Notes:

Notes:

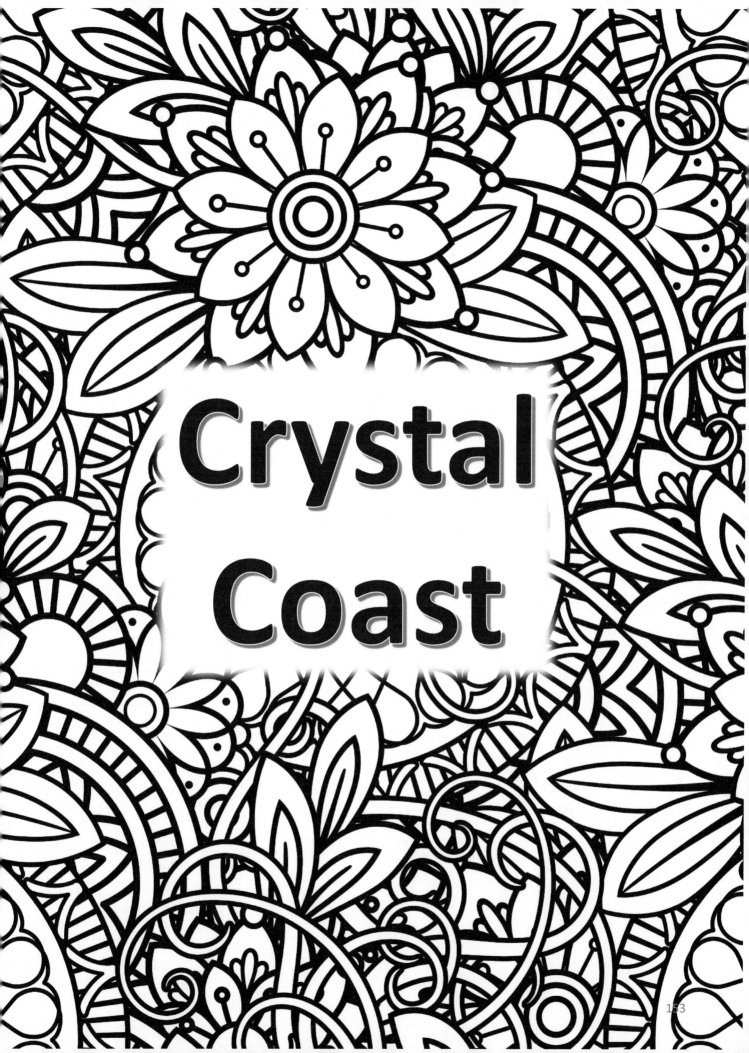

Cedar Island

City: Cedar Island   County: Carteret

Plan your trip: https://www.crystalcoast.com/cedar-island-guide.html

Activities:

- ❑ Biking
- ❑ Boating
- ❑ Disc Golf
- ❑ Fishing
- ❑ Gold Panning
- ❑ Hiking
- ❑ Historic Learning
- ❑ Horseback Riding
- ❑ Hunting
- ❑ Kite Boarding

- ❑ Metal Detecting
- ❑ OHV
- ❑ Paddling
- ❑ Rock Climbing
- ❑ Stargazing
- ❑ Swimming
- ❑ Wildlife Viewing
- ❑ Windsurfing
- ❑
- ❑

- ❑
- ❑
- ❑
- ❑
- ❑
- ❑
- ❑
- ❑
- ❑
- ❑

Facilities:

- ❑ ADA
- ❑ Picnic sites
- ❑ Restrooms
- ❑ Showers
- ❑ Trailer Access
- ❑ Visitor center
- ❑ Group Camping
- ❑ RV Camp
- ❑ Rustic Camping
- ❑ Cabins / Yurts
- ❑ Day Use Area

Notes:

Get the Facts

- ❑ Phone
- ❑ Park Hours

  _____

- ❑ Reservations? ____Y ____N

  date made_____

- ❑ Open all year ____Y____N

  dates_____

- ❑ Check in time _____
- ❑ Check out time _____
- ❑ Pet friendly _____Y _____N
- ❑ Max RV length _____
- ❑ Distance from home

  miles: _____

  hours: _____

- ❑ Address_____

  _____

  _____

Fees:

- ❑ Day Use $ _____
- ❑ Camp Sites $ _____
- ❑ RV Sites $ _____
- ❑ Refund policy

  _____

  _____

  _____

Make It Personal

Trip dates: _____

The weather was: Sunny Cloudy Rainy Stormy Snowy Foggy Warm Cold

Why I went:
_____

How I got there: (circle all that apply) Plane Train Car Bus Bike Hike RV MC

I went with:
_____

We stayed in (space, cabin # etc):
_____

Most relaxing day:
_____

Something funny:
_____

Someone we met:
_____

Best story told:
_____

The kids liked this:
_____

The best food:
_____

Games played:
_____

Something disappointing:
_____

Next time I'll do this differently:
_____
_____

Harkers Island
City: Harkers Island   County: Carteret
Plan your trip: https://www.crystalcoast.com/harkers-island.html

Activities:

- ☐ Biking
- ☐ Boating
- ☐ Disc Golf
- ☐ Fishing
- ☐ Gold Panning
- ☐ Hiking
- ☐ Historic Learning
- ☐ Horseback Riding
- ☐ Hunting
- ☐ Kite Boarding
- ☐ Metal Detecting
- ☐ OHV
- ☐ Paddling
- ☐ Rock Climbing
- ☐ Stargazing
- ☐ Swimming
- ☐ Wildlife Viewing
- ☐ Windsurfing
- ☐
- ☐
- ☐
- ☐
- ☐
- ☐
- ☐
- ☐
- ☐
- ☐
- ☐
- ☐

Facilities:

- ☐ ADA
- ☐ Picnic sites
- ☐ Restrooms
- ☐ Showers
- ☐ Trailer Access
- ☐ Visitor center
- ☐ Group Camping
- ☐ RV Camp
- ☐ Rustic Camping
- ☐ Cabins / Yurts
- ☐ Day Use Area

Notes:

Get the Facts

- ☐ Phone
- ☐ Park Hours

  _____

- ☐ Reservations? ____Y ____N

  date made_____
- ☐ Open all year ____Y____N

  dates_____
- ☐ Check in time _____
- ☐ Check out time _____
- ☐ Pet friendly _____Y _____N
- ☐ Max RV length _____
- ☐ Distance from home

  miles: _____

  hours: _____
- ☐ Address_____

  _____

  _____

Fees:

- ☐ Day Use $ _____
- ☐ Camp Sites $ _____
- ☐ RV Sites $ _____
- ☐ Refund policy

  _____

  _____

  _____

Make It Personal

Trip dates:

The weather was: Sunny Cloudy Rainy Stormy Snowy Foggy Warm Cold

Why I went:

How I got there: (circle all that apply) Plane Train Car Bus Bike Hike RV MC

I went with:

We stayed in (space, cabin # etc):

Most relaxing day:

Something funny:

Someone we met:

Best story told:

The kids liked this:

The best food:

Games played:

Something disappointing:

Next time I'll do this differently:

Beaufort

City: Beaufort   County: Carteret

Plan your trip: https://www.beaufort-nc.com/

Activities:

- ☐ Biking
- ☐ Boating
- ☐ Disc Golf
- ☐ Fishing
- ☐ Gold Panning
- ☐ Hiking
- ☐ Historic Learning
- ☐ Horseback Riding
- ☐ Hunting
- ☐ Kite Boarding
- ☐ Metal Detecting
- ☐ OHV
- ☐ Paddling
- ☐ Rock Climbing
- ☐ Stargazing
- ☐ Swimming
- ☐ Wildlife Viewing
- ☐ Windsurfing
- ☐
- ☐
- ☐
- ☐
- ☐
- ☐
- ☐
- ☐
- ☐
- ☐
- ☐
- ☐
- ☐

Facilities:

- ☐ ADA
- ☐ Picnic sites
- ☐ Restrooms
- ☐ Showers
- ☐ Trailer Access
- ☐ Visitor center
- ☐ Group Camping
- ☐ RV Camp
- ☐ Rustic Camping
- ☐ Cabins / Yurts
- ☐ Day Use Area

Notes:

Get the Facts

- ☐ Phone   252-728-5225
- ☐ Park Hours

  _____

- ☐ Reservations? ____Y ____N

  date made_____

- ☐ Open all year ____Y____N

  dates_____

- ☐ Check in time _____
- ☐ Check out time _____
- ☐ Pet friendly _____Y _____N
- ☐ Max RV length _____
- ☐ Distance from home

  miles: _____

  hours: _____

- ☐ Address_____

  _____

  _____

Fees:

- ☐ Day Use $ _____
- ☐ Camp Sites $ _____
- ☐ RV Sites $ _____
- ☐ Refund policy

  _____

  _____

  _____

Make It Personal

Trip dates:

The weather was: Sunny Cloudy Rainy Stormy Snowy Foggy Warm Cold

Why I went:

How I got there: (circle all that apply) Plane Train Car Bus Bike Hike RV MC

I went with:

We stayed in (space, cabin # etc):

Most relaxing day:

Something funny:

Someone we met:

Best story told:

The kids liked this:

The best food:

Games played:

Something disappointing:

Next time I'll do this differently:

Morehead City
City: Morehead City   County: Carteret

Plan your trip: https://www.morehead.com/

Activities:

- ❑ Biking
- ❑ Boating
- ❑ Disc Golf
- ❑ Fishing
- ❑ Gold Panning
- ❑ Hiking
- ❑ Historic Learning
- ❑ Horseback Riding
- ❑ Hunting
- ❑ Kite Boarding
- ❑ Metal Detecting
- ❑ OHV
- ❑ Paddling
- ❑ Rock Climbing
- ❑ Stargazing
- ❑ Swimming
- ❑ Wildlife Viewing
- ❑ Windsurfing
- ❑
- ❑
- ❑
- ❑
- ❑
- ❑
- ❑
- ❑
- ❑
- ❑
- ❑
- ❑

Facilities:

- ❑ ADA
- ❑ Picnic sites
- ❑ Restrooms
- ❑ Showers
- ❑ Trailer Access
- ❑ Visitor center
- ❑ Group Camping
- ❑ RV Camp
- ❑ Rustic Camping
- ❑ Cabins / Yurts
- ❑ Day Use Area

Notes:

Get the Facts

- ❑ Phone   252-728-5225
- ❑ Park Hours
  _____
- ❑ Reservations? ____Y ____N
  date made_____
- ❑ Open all year ____Y____N
  dates_____
- ❑ Check in time _____
- ❑ Check out time _____
- ❑ Pet friendly _____Y _____N
- ❑ Max RV length _____
- ❑ Distance from home
  miles: _____
  hours: _____
- ❑ Address_____
  _____
  _____

Fees:

- ❑ Day Use $ _____
- ❑ Camp Sites $ _____
- ❑ RV Sites $ _____
- ❑ Refund policy
  _____
  _____
  _____

Make It Personal

Trip dates:

The weather was: Sunny Cloudy Rainy Stormy Snowy Foggy Warm Cold

Why I went:

How I got there: (circle all that apply) Plane Train Car Bus Bike Hike RV MC

I went with:

We stayed in (space, cabin # etc):

Most relaxing day:

Something funny:

Someone we met:

Best story told:

The kids liked this:

The best food:

Games played:

Something disappointing:

Next time I'll do this differently:

Emerald Isle
City: Emerald Isle   County: Carteret
Plan your trip: https://www.crystalcoastnc.org/region/emerald-isle/

Activities:

- ❑ Biking
- ❑ Boating
- ❑ Disc Golf
- ❑ Fishing
- ❑ Gold Panning
- ❑ Hiking
- ❑ Historic Learning
- ❑ Horseback Riding
- ❑ Hunting
- ❑ Kite Boarding
- ❑ Metal Detecting
- ❑ OHV
- ❑ Paddling
- ❑ Rock Climbing
- ❑ Stargazing
- ❑ Swimming
- ❑ Wildlife Viewing
- ❑ Windsurfing
- ❑
- ❑
- ❑
- ❑
- ❑
- ❑
- ❑
- ❑
- ❑
- ❑
- ❑
- ❑

Facilities:

- ❑ ADA
- ❑ Picnic sites
- ❑ Restrooms
- ❑ Showers
- ❑ Trailer Access
- ❑ Visitor center
- ❑ Group Camping
- ❑ RV Camp
- ❑ Rustic Camping
- ❑ Cabins / Yurts
- ❑ Day Use Area

Notes:

Get the Facts

- ❑ Phone   252-354-3424
- ❑ Park Hours

  _____

- ❑ Reservations? ____Y ____N

  date made_____
- ❑ Open all year ____Y____N

  dates_____
- ❑ Check in time _____
- ❑ Check out time _____
- ❑ Pet friendly _____Y _____N
- ❑ Max RV length _____
- ❑ Distance from home

  miles: _____

  hours: _____
- ❑ Address_____

  _____

  _____

Fees:

- ❑ Day Use $ _____
- ❑ Camp Sites $ _____
- ❑ RV Sites $ _____
- ❑ Refund policy

  _____

  _____

  _____

Make It Personal

Trip dates: _____

The weather was: Sunny Cloudy Rainy Stormy Snowy Foggy Warm Cold

Why I went:
_____

How I got there: (circle all that apply) Plane Train Car Bus Bike Hike RV MC

I went with:
_____

We stayed in (space, cabin # etc):
_____

Most relaxing day:
_____

Something funny:
_____

Someone we met:
_____

Best story told:
_____

The kids liked this:
_____

The best food:
_____

Games played:
_____

Something disappointing:
_____

Next time I'll do this differently:
_____

Cape Lookout National Seashore
City: Harkers Island   County: Carteret

Plan your trip: https://www.nps.gov/calo/index.htm

Activities:

- ❑ ATV / OHV   ❑
- ❑ Bike Trails   ❑
- ❑ Birding   ❑
- ❑ Boating   ❑
- ❑ Fishing   ❑
- ❑ Hiking   ❑
- ❑ Horseback   ❑
- ❑ Mountain Biking ❑
- ❑ Watersports   ❑
- ❑ Wildlife   ❑
- ❑ Winter Sports

Facilities:

- ❑ ADA   ❑
- ❑ Gift Shop   ❑
- ❑ Museum   ❑
- ❑ Visitor Center   ❑
- ❑ Picnic sites   ❑
- ❑ Restrooms   ❑

Things to do in the area:

Get the Facts

- ❑ Phone   252-728-2250
- ❑ Park Hours

  _____

- ❑ Reservations? ____Y ____N

  date made_____

- ❑ Open all year? ____Y____N

  dates_____

- ❑ Dog friendly _____Y _____N

- ❑ Distance from home

  miles: _____

  hours: _____

- ❑ Address_____

  _____

  _____

Fees:

- ❑ Day Use $ _____
- ❑ Refund policy

  _____

  _____

  _____

Notes:

Shackleford Banks
City: Harkers Island   County: Carteret
Plan your trip: https://www.outerbanks.com/shackleford-banks.html

Activities:

- ❑ ATV / OHV   ❑
- ❑ Bike Trails   ❑
- ❑ Birding   ❑
- ❑ Boating   ❑
- ❑ Fishing   ❑
- ❑ Hiking   ❑
- ❑ Horseback   ❑
- ❑ Mountain Biking   ❑
- ❑ Watersports   ❑
- ❑ Wildlife   ❑
- ❑ Winter Sports

Facilities:

- ❑ ADA   ❑
- ❑ Gift Shop   ❑
- ❑ Museum   ❑
- ❑ Visitor Center   ❑
- ❑ Picnic sites   ❑
- ❑ Restrooms   ❑

Things to do in the area:

Get the Facts

- ❑ Phone
- ❑ Park Hours

  _____

- ❑ Reservations? ____Y ____N

  date made_____

- ❑ Open all year? ____Y____N

  dates_____

- ❑ Dog friendly _____Y _____N

- ❑ Distance from home

  miles: _____

  hours: _____

- ❑ Address_____

  _____

  _____

Fees:

- ❑ Day Use $ _____
- ❑ Refund policy

  _____

  _____

  _____

Notes:

Fort Macon State Park
City: Atlantic Beach   County: Carteret

Plan your trip: https://www.ncparks.gov/fort-macon-state-park/home

Activities:

- ❏ ATV / OHV   ❏
- ❏ Bike Trails   ❏
- ❏ Birding   ❏
- ❏ Boating   ❏
- ❏ Fishing   ❏
- ❏ Hiking   ❏
- ❏ Horseback   ❏
- ❏ Mountain Biking   ❏
- ❏ Watersports   ❏
- ❏ Wildlife   ❏
- ❏ Winter Sports

Facilities:

- ❏ ADA   ❏
- ❏ Gift Shop   ❏
- ❏ Museum   ❏
- ❏ Visitor Center   ❏
- ❏ Picnic sites   ❏
- ❏ Restrooms   ❏

Things to do in the area:

Get the Facts

- ❏ Phone 252-726-3775
- ❏ Park Hours

_____

- ❏ Reservations? _____Y _____N

date made_____

- ❏ Open all year? _____Y_____N

dates_____

- ❏ Dog friendly _____Y _____N

- ❏ Distance from home

miles: _____

hours: _____

- ❏ Address_____

_____

_____

Fees:

- ❏ Day Use $ _____
- ❏ Refund policy

_____

_____

_____

Notes:

Atlantic Beach
City: Atlantic Beach   County: Carteret
Plan your trip: http://atlanticbeach-nc.com/

Activities:

- ❑ ATV / OHV   ❑
- ❑ Bike Trails   ❑
- ❑ Birding   ❑
- ❑ Boating   ❑
- ❑ Fishing   ❑
- ❑ Hiking   ❑
- ❑ Horseback   ❑
- ❑ Mountain Biking   ❑
- ❑ Watersports   ❑
- ❑ Wildlife   ❑
- ❑ Winter Sports

Facilities:

- ❑ ADA   ❑
- ❑ Gift Shop   ❑
- ❑ Museum   ❑
- ❑ Visitor Center   ❑
- ❑ Picnic sites   ❑
- ❑ Restrooms   ❑

Things to do in the area:

Get the Facts

- ❑ Phone   252-726-2121
- ❑ Park Hours

  _____

- ❑ Reservations? _____Y _____N

  date made_____

- ❑ Open all year? _____Y_____N

  dates_____

- ❑ Dog friendly _____Y _____N

- ❑ Distance from home

  miles: _____

  hours: _____

- ❑ Address_____

  _____

  _____

Fees:

- ❑ Day Use $ _____
- ❑ Refund policy

  _____

  _____

  _____

Notes:

Pine Knoll Shores
City: Pine Knoll Shores   County: Carteret
Plan your trip: https://www.townofpks.com/

Activities:

- [ ] ATV / OHV   [ ]
- [ ] Bike Trails   [ ]
- [ ] Birding   [ ]
- [ ] Boating   [ ]
- [ ] Fishing   [ ]
- [ ] Hiking   [ ]
- [ ] Horseback   [ ]
- [ ] Mountain Biking   [ ]
- [ ] Watersports   [ ]
- [ ] Wildlife   [ ]
- [ ] Winter Sports

Facilities:

- [ ] ADA   [ ]
- [ ] Gift Shop   [ ]
- [ ] Museum   [ ]
- [ ] Visitor Center   [ ]
- [ ] Picnic sites   [ ]
- [ ] Restrooms   [ ]

Things to do in the area:

Get the Facts

- [ ] Phone   252-247 4353
- [ ] Park Hours

  _____

- [ ] Reservations? ____Y ____N

  date made_____

- [ ] Open all year? ____Y____N

  dates_____

- [ ] Dog friendly _____Y _____N

- [ ] Distance from home

  miles: _____

  hours: _____

- [ ] Address_____

  _____

  _____

Fees:

- [ ] Day Use $ _____
- [ ] Refund policy

  _____

  _____

  _____

Notes:

Theodore Roosevelt Natural Area
City: Pine Knoll Shores   County: Carteret
Plan your trip: http://www.ncnatural.com/Coast/naturalsouth.html

Activities:

- ❏ ATV / OHV   ❏
- ❏ Bike Trails   ❏
- ❏ Birding   ❏
- ❏ Boating   ❏
- ❏ Fishing   ❏
- ❏ Hiking   ❏
- ❏ Horseback   ❏
- ❏ Mountain Biking   ❏
- ❏ Watersports   ❏
- ❏ Wildlife   ❏
- ❏ Winter Sports

Facilities:

- ❏ ADA   ❏
- ❏ Gift Shop   ❏
- ❏ Museum   ❏
- ❏ Visitor Center   ❏
- ❏ Picnic sites   ❏
- ❏ Restrooms   ❏

Things to do in the area:

Get the Facts

- ❏ Phone   252-726-3775
- ❏ Park Hours

  _____

- ❏ Reservations? _____Y _____N

  date made_____

- ❏ Open all year? _____Y_____N

  dates_____

- ❏ Dog friendly _____Y _____N

- ❏ Distance from home

  miles: _____

  hours: _____

- ❏ Address_____

  _____

  _____

Fees:

- ❏ Day Use $ _____
- ❏ Refund policy

  _____

  _____

  _____

Notes:

Indian Beach
City: Indian Beach   County: Carteret
Plan your trip: https://www.crystalcoastnc.org/region/indian-beach/

Activities:

- ❑ ATV / OHV   ❑
- ❑ Bike Trails   ❑
- ❑ Birding   ❑
- ❑ Boating   ❑
- ❑ Fishing   ❑
- ❑ Hiking   ❑
- ❑ Horseback   ❑
- ❑ Mountain Biking   ❑
- ❑ Watersports   ❑
- ❑ Wildlife   ❑
- ❑ Winter Sports

Facilities:

- ❑ ADA   ❑
- ❑ Gift Shop   ❑
- ❑ Museum   ❑
- ❑ Visitor Center   ❑
- ❑ Picnic sites   ❑
- ❑ Restrooms   ❑

Things to do in the area:

Get the Facts

- ❑ Phone   252-247-3344
- ❑ Park Hours

  _____

- ❑ Reservations? ____Y ____N

  date made_____

- ❑ Open all year? ____Y____N

  dates_____

- ❑ Dog friendly _____Y _____N

- ❑ Distance from home

  miles: _____

  hours: _____

- ❑ Address_____

  _____

  _____

Fees:

- ❑ Day Use $ _____
- ❑ Refund policy

  _____

  _____

  _____

Notes:

Name:
City: County:

Plan your trip:

Activities:

- ❏ ATV / OHV   ❏
- ❏ Bike Trails   ❏
- ❏ Birding   ❏
- ❏ Boating   ❏
- ❏ Fishing   ❏
- ❏ Hiking   ❏
- ❏ Horseback   ❏
- ❏ Mountain Biking ❏
- ❏ Watersports   ❏
- ❏ Wildlife   ❏
- ❏ Winter Sports

Facilities:

- ❏ ADA   ❏
- ❏ Gift Shop   ❏
- ❏ Museum   ❏
- ❏ Visitor Center   ❏
- ❏ Picnic sites   ❏
- ❏ Restrooms   ❏

Things to do in the area:

Get the Facts

- ❏ Phone _____
- ❏ Park Hours

  _____

- ❏ Reservations? ____Y ____N

  date made_____

- ❏ Open all year? ____Y____N

  dates_____

- ❏ Dog friendly _____Y _____N

- ❏ Distance from home

  miles: _____

  hours: _____

- ❏ Address_____

  _____

  _____

Fees:

- ❏ Day Use $ _____
- ❏ Refund policy

  _____

  _____

  _____

Notes:

Name:
City: County:
Plan your trip:

Activities:

- [ ] ATV / OHV   [ ]
- [ ] Bike Trails   [ ]
- [ ] Birding   [ ]
- [ ] Boating   [ ]
- [ ] Fishing   [ ]
- [ ] Hiking   [ ]
- [ ] Horseback   [ ]
- [ ] Mountain Biking   [ ]
- [ ] Watersports   [ ]
- [ ] Wildlife   [ ]
- [ ] Winter Sports

Facilities:

- [ ] ADA   [ ]
- [ ] Gift Shop   [ ]
- [ ] Museum   [ ]
- [ ] Visitor Center   [ ]
- [ ] Picnic sites   [ ]
- [ ] Restrooms   [ ]

Things to do in the area:

Get the Facts

- [ ] Phone _____
- [ ] Park Hours

  _____

- [ ] Reservations? ____Y ____N

  date made_____
- [ ] Open all year? ____Y____N

  dates_____
- [ ] Dog friendly _____Y _____N
- [ ] Distance from home

  miles: _____

  hours: _____
- [ ] Address_____

  _____

  _____

Fees:

- [ ] Day Use $ _____
- [ ] Refund policy

  _____

  _____

  _____

Notes:

Name:
City: ## County:
Plan your trip:

Activities:

- ❑ ATV / OHV   ❑
- ❑ Bike Trails   ❑
- ❑ Birding   ❑
- ❑ Boating   ❑
- ❑ Fishing   ❑
- ❑ Hiking   ❑
- ❑ Horseback   ❑
- ❑ Mountain Biking   ❑
- ❑ Watersports   ❑
- ❑ Wildlife   ❑
- ❑ Winter Sports

Facilities:

- ❑ ADA   ❑
- ❑ Gift Shop   ❑
- ❑ Museum   ❑
- ❑ Visitor Center   ❑
- ❑ Picnic sites   ❑
- ❑ Restrooms   ❑

Things to do in the area:

Get the Facts

- ❑ Phone _____
- ❑ Park Hours

    _____

- ❑ Reservations? ____Y ____N

    date made_____

- ❑ Open all year? ____Y____N

    dates_____

- ❑ Dog friendly _____Y _____N

- ❑ Distance from home

    miles: _____

    hours: _____

- ❑ Address_____

    _____

    _____

Fees:

- ❑ Day Use $ _____
- ❑ Refund policy

    _____

    _____

    _____

Notes:

Name:
City: County:
Plan your trip:

Activities:

- ☐ ATV / OHV   ☐
- ☐ Bike Trails   ☐
- ☐ Birding   ☐
- ☐ Boating   ☐
- ☐ Fishing   ☐
- ☐ Hiking   ☐
- ☐ Horseback   ☐
- ☐ Mountain Biking   ☐
- ☐ Watersports   ☐
- ☐ Wildlife   ☐
- ☐ Winter Sports

Facilities:

- ☐ ADA   ☐
- ☐ Gift Shop   ☐
- ☐ Museum   ☐
- ☐ Visitor Center   ☐
- ☐ Picnic sites   ☐
- ☐ Restrooms   ☐

Things to do in the area:

Get the Facts

- ☐ Phone _____
- ☐ Park Hours

  _____

- ☐ Reservations? ____Y ____N

  date made_____

- ☐ Open all year? ____Y____N

  dates_____

- ☐ Dog friendly _____Y _____N

- ☐ Distance from home

  miles: _____

  hours: _____

- ☐ Address_____

  _____

  _____

Fees:

- ☐ Day Use $ _____
- ☐ Refund policy

  _____

  _____

  _____

Notes:

Name:
City: County:
Plan your trip:

Activities:

- [ ] ATV / OHV   [ ]
- [ ] Bike Trails   [ ]
- [ ] Birding   [ ]
- [ ] Boating   [ ]
- [ ] Fishing   [ ]
- [ ] Hiking   [ ]
- [ ] Horseback   [ ]
- [ ] Mountain Biking   [ ]
- [ ] Watersports   [ ]
- [ ] Wildlife   [ ]
- [ ] Winter Sports

Facilities:

- [ ] ADA   [ ]
- [ ] Gift Shop   [ ]
- [ ] Museum   [ ]
- [ ] Visitor Center   [ ]
- [ ] Picnic sites   [ ]
- [ ] Restrooms   [ ]

Things to do in the area:

Get the Facts

- [ ] Phone _____
- [ ] Park Hours

  _____

- [ ] Reservations? ____Y ____N

  date made_____

- [ ] Open all year? ____Y____N

  dates_____

- [ ] Dog friendly _____Y _____N
- [ ] Distance from home

  miles: _____

  hours: _____

- [ ] Address_____

  _____

  _____

Fees:

- [ ] Day Use $ _____
- [ ] Refund policy

  _____

  _____

  _____

Notes:

Name:
City: County:
Plan your trip:

Activities:

- ❑ ATV / OHV   ❑
- ❑ Bike Trails   ❑
- ❑ Birding   ❑
- ❑ Boating   ❑
- ❑ Fishing   ❑
- ❑ Hiking   ❑
- ❑ Horseback   ❑
- ❑ Mountain Biking   ❑
- ❑ Watersports   ❑
- ❑ Wildlife   ❑
- ❑ Winter Sports

Facilities:

- ❑ ADA   ❑
- ❑ Gift Shop   ❑
- ❑ Museum   ❑
- ❑ Visitor Center   ❑
- ❑ Picnic sites   ❑
- ❑ Restrooms   ❑

Things to do in the area:

Get the Facts

- ❑ Phone _____
- ❑ Park Hours

  _____

- ❑ Reservations? ____Y ____N

  date made_____

- ❑ Open all year? ____Y____N

  dates_____

- ❑ Dog friendly _____Y _____N

- ❑ Distance from home

  miles: _____

  hours: _____

- ❑ Address_____

  _____

  _____

Fees:

- ❑ Day Use $ _____
- ❑ Refund policy

  _____

  _____

  _____

Notes:

Name:
City: County:

Plan your trip:

Activities:

- ❑ ATV / OHV   ❑
- ❑ Bike Trails   ❑
- ❑ Birding   ❑
- ❑ Boating   ❑
- ❑ Fishing   ❑
- ❑ Hiking   ❑
- ❑ Horseback   ❑
- ❑ Mountain Biking   ❑
- ❑ Watersports   ❑
- ❑ Wildlife   ❑
- ❑ Winter Sports

Facilities:

- ❑ ADA   ❑
- ❑ Gift Shop   ❑
- ❑ Museum   ❑
- ❑ Visitor Center   ❑
- ❑ Picnic sites   ❑
- ❑ Restrooms   ❑

Things to do in the area:

Get the Facts

- ❑ Phone _____
- ❑ Park Hours

  _____

- ❑ Reservations? ____Y ____N

  date made_____

- ❑ Open all year? ____Y____N

  dates_____

- ❑ Dog friendly _____Y _____N

- ❑ Distance from home

  miles: _____

  hours: _____

- ❑ Address_____

  _____

  _____

Fees:

- ❑ Day Use $ _____
- ❑ Refund policy

  _____

  _____

  _____

Notes:

Name:

City: County:

Plan your trip:

Activities:

- ❑ Biking
- ❑ Boating
- ❑ Disc Golf
- ❑ Fishing
- ❑ Gold Panning
- ❑ Hiking
- ❑ Historic Learning
- ❑ Horseback Riding
- ❑ Hunting
- ❑ Kite Boarding

- ❑ Metal Detecting
- ❑ OHV
- ❑ Paddling
- ❑ Rock Climbing
- ❑ Stargazing
- ❑ Swimming
- ❑ Wildlife Viewing
- ❑ Windsurfing
- ❑
- ❑

- ❑
- ❑
- ❑
- ❑
- ❑
- ❑
- ❑
- ❑
- ❑
- ❑
- ❑
- ❑

Facilities:

- ❑ ADA
- ❑ Picnic sites
- ❑ Restrooms
- ❑ Showers
- ❑ Trailer Access
- ❑ Visitor center
- ❑ Group Camping
- ❑ RV Camp
- ❑ Rustic Camping
- ❑ Cabins / Yurts
- ❑ Day Use Area

Notes:

Get the Facts

- ❑ Phone_____
- ❑ Park Hours

  _____

- ❑ Reservations? ____Y ____N

  date made_____

- ❑ Open all year ____Y_____N

  dates_____

- ❑ Check in time _____
- ❑ Check out time _____
- ❑ Pet friendly _____Y _____N
- ❑ Max RV length _____
- ❑ Distance from home

  miles: _____

  hours: _____

- ❑ Address_____

  _____

  _____

Fees:

- ❑ Day Use $ _____
- ❑ Camp Sites $ _____
- ❑ RV Sites $ _____
- ❑ Refund policy

  _____

  _____

  _____

Make It Personal

Trip dates:

The weather was: Sunny Cloudy Rainy Stormy Snowy Foggy Warm Cold

Why I went:

How I got there: (circle all that apply) Plane Train Car Bus Bike Hike RV MC

I went with:

We stayed in (space, cabin # etc):

Most relaxing day:

Something funny:

Someone we met:

Best story told:

The kids liked this:

The best food:

Games played:

Something disappointing:

Next time I'll do this differently:

Name:

City: County:

Plan your trip:

Activities:

- ❑ Biking
- ❑ Boating
- ❑ Disc Golf
- ❑ Fishing
- ❑ Gold Panning
- ❑ Hiking
- ❑ Historic Learning
- ❑ Horseback Riding
- ❑ Hunting
- ❑ Kite Boarding

- ❑ Metal Detecting
- ❑ OHV
- ❑ Paddling
- ❑ Rock Climbing
- ❑ Stargazing
- ❑ Swimming
- ❑ Wildlife Viewing
- ❑ Windsurfing
- ❑
- ❑

- ❑
- ❑
- ❑
- ❑
- ❑
- ❑
- ❑
- ❑
- ❑
- ❑

Facilities:

- ❑ ADA
- ❑ Picnic sites
- ❑ Restrooms
- ❑ Showers
- ❑ Trailer Access
- ❑ Visitor center
- ❑ Group Camping
- ❑ RV Camp
- ❑ Rustic Camping
- ❑ Cabins / Yurts
- ❑ Day Use Area

Notes:

Get the Facts

- ❑ Phone_____
- ❑ Park Hours

  _____

- ❑ Reservations? _____Y _____N

  date made_____

- ❑ Open all year _____Y_____N

  dates_____

- ❑ Check in time _____
- ❑ Check out time _____
- ❑ Pet friendly _____Y _____N
- ❑ Max RV length _____
- ❑ Distance from home

  miles: _____

  hours: _____

- ❑ Address_____

  _____

  _____

Fees:

- ❑ Day Use $ _____
- ❑ Camp Sites $ _____
- ❑ RV Sites $ _____
- ❑ Refund policy

  _____

  _____

  _____

Make It Personal

Trip dates: _____ | The weather was: Sunny Cloudy Rainy Stormy Snowy Foggy Warm Cold

Why I went:
_____

How I got there: (circle all that apply) Plane Train Car Bus Bike Hike RV MC

I went with:
_____

We stayed in (space, cabin # etc):
_____

Most relaxing day:
_____

Something funny:
_____

Someone we met:
_____

Best story told:
_____

The kids liked this:
_____

The best food:
_____

Games played:
_____

Something disappointing:
_____

Next time I'll do this differently:
_____
_____

Name:

City: County:

Plan your trip:

Activities:

- ❑ Biking
- ❑ Boating
- ❑ Disc Golf
- ❑ Fishing
- ❑ Gold Panning
- ❑ Hiking
- ❑ Historic Learning
- ❑ Horseback Riding
- ❑ Hunting
- ❑ Kite Boarding

- ❑ Metal Detecting
- ❑ OHV
- ❑ Paddling
- ❑ Rock Climbing
- ❑ Stargazing
- ❑ Swimming
- ❑ Wildlife Viewing
- ❑ Windsurfing
- ❑
- ❑

- ❑
- ❑
- ❑
- ❑
- ❑
- ❑
- ❑
- ❑
- ❑
- ❑

Facilities:

- ❑ ADA
- ❑ Picnic sites
- ❑ Restrooms
- ❑ Showers
- ❑ Trailer Access
- ❑ Visitor center
- ❑ Group Camping
- ❑ RV Camp
- ❑ Rustic Camping
- ❑ Cabins / Yurts
- ❑ Day Use Area

Notes:

Get the Facts

- ❑ Phone_____
- ❑ Park Hours

  _____

- ❑ Reservations? ____Y ____N

  date made_____

- ❑ Open all year ____Y____N

  dates_____

- ❑ Check in time _____
- ❑ Check out time _____
- ❑ Pet friendly _____Y _____N
- ❑ Max RV length _____
- ❑ Distance from home

  miles: _____

  hours: _____

- ❑ Address_____

  _____

  _____

Fees:

- ❑ Day Use $ _____
- ❑ Camp Sites $ _____
- ❑ RV Sites $ _____
- ❑ Refund policy

  _____

  _____

  _____

Make It Personal

Trip dates: | The weather was: Sunny Cloudy Rainy Stormy Snowy Foggy Warm Cold

Why I went:

How I got there: (circle all that apply) Plane Train Car Bus Bike Hike RV MC

I went with:

We stayed in (space, cabin # etc):

Most relaxing day:

Something funny:

Someone we met:

Best story told:

The kids liked this:

The best food:

Games played:

Something disappointing:

Next time I'll do this differently:

INDEX

- Alamance Battleground Historic Site...... 107
- Atlantic Beach... 167
- Avon Beach... 147
- Battleship North Carolina Historic Site... 36
- Beaufort.. 158
- Bennett Place Historic Site........................ 104
- Bentonville Battlefield Historic Site........ 111
- Biltmore Estate.. 46
- Bladen Lakes State Forest............................ 10
- Bodie Island Lighthouse............................ 144
- Boones Cave Park... 70
- Brunswick Town / Fort Anderson HS....... 27
- Buxton Beach.. 126
- Cape Hatteras Lighthouse.......................... 148
- Cape Hatteras National Seashore.............143
- Cape Lookout National Seashore.............164
- Carolina Beach State Park........................... 20
- Carova Beach.. 132
- Carvers Creek State Park............................ 103
- Cedar Island.. 154
- Charlotte Hawkins Brown Museum HS... 108
- Chimney Rock State Park............................. 62
- Cliffs of the Neuse State Park.................... 100
- Corolla Beach.. 135
- Crowders Mountain State Park.................... 66
- CSS Neuse & Gov. Caswell Memorial Historic Site... 33
- Currituck Beach Lighthouse...................... 134
- Currituck National Wildlife Refuge.......... 133
- Dismal Swamp State Park............................. 28
- Duck Beach... 136
- Duke Homestead Historic Site................. 105
- Elk Knob State Park...................................... 58
- Emerald Isle.. 162
- Eno River State Park..................................... 42
- Falls Lake State Recreation Area............... 98
- Fort Dobbs Historic Site............................ 110
- Fort Fisher State Recreation Area............. 34
- Fort Fisher State Historic Site.................... 35
- Fort Macon State Park................................ 166
- Frisco Beach.. 128
- Goose Creek State Park................................. 8
- Gorges State Park... 52
- Governor Charles B. Aycock Birthplace Historic Site.. 120
- Grandfather Mountain State Park............. 44
- Hammocks Beach State Park....................... 22
- Hanging Rock State Park.............................. 68
- Harkers Island... 156
- Hatteras Beach.. 149
- Haw River State Park.................................... 76
- Historic Bath... 26
- Historic Edenton... 29
- Historic Halifax... 109
- Historic Stagville Historic Site................. 106
- Horne Creek Farm Historic Site.............. 118
- House in the Horseshoe Historic Site... 112
- Indian Beach.. 170
- Jockeys Ridge State Park............................. 32
- Jones Lake State Park.................................... 12
- Jordan Lake State Recreation Area........... 94
- Julian Price Memorial Park......................... 54
- Kerr Lake State Recreation Area............... 92
- Kill Devil Hills... 139
- Kitty Hawk Woods Coastal Reserve...... 138
- Lake James State Park.................................. 50
- Lake Norman State Park.............................. 82
- Lake Waccamaw State Park......................... 16
- Little River Regional Park/Natural Area.. 74
- Lumber River State Park............................. 84
- Manteo Island..141
- Mayo River State Park................................. 86
- Medoc Mountain State Park....................... 78
- Merchants Millpond State Park.............. 18
- Morehead City...160
- Morrow Mountain State Park.................... 88
- Moses H Cone Memorial Park.................... 63
- Mount Jefferson State Park.........................59
- Mount Mitchell State Park...........................56
- Nags Head Beach..140
- New River State Park.................................... 40
- North Carolina State Capitol.....................119
- North Carolina Transportation Museum.. 117
- Occoneechee Mountain State Natural Area... 116
- Ocracoke Beach... 130
- Orcacoke Lighthouse................................. 150
- Pea Island National Wildlife Refuge...... 145
- Pettigrew State Park..................................... 24
- Pilot Mountain State Park........................... 90
- Pine Knoll Shores....................................... 168
- Portsmouth Island...................................... 151

INDEX

- President James K. Polk Historic Site.......113
- Raven Rock State Park............................ 80
- Reed Gold Mine Historic Site.................. 102
- Rendezvous Mountain Educational State Forest................................ 64
- Roanoke Island Festival Park HS.............. 31
- Rodanthe Beach...122
- Salvo Day Use Area.................................. 146
- Shackleford Banks................................... 165
- Singletary Lake State Park....................... 14
- Somerset Place Historic Site.................... 37
- South Mountains State Park.................... 48
- Southern Shores Beach.............................137
- Stone Mountain State Park....................... 42
- Theodore Roosevelt Natural Area...........169
- Thomas Wolfe Memorial Historic Site...... 60
- Town Creek Indian Mound HS.................. 114
- Tryon Palace Historic Site......................... 30
- Wanchese Island.......................................142
- Waves Beach... 124
- Weymouth Woods Sandhills Nature Preserve.......................................115
- William B Umstead State Park.................. 96
- Zebulon B. Vance Birthplace HS.............. 61